More Praise for
Measurement and Evaluation on a Shoestring

"Alaina offers a generous smorgasbord of concepts, principles, methods, tips, and tools that L&D practitioners can use fruitfully to plan, practice, and most importantly, leverage the impact of measurement and evaluation to increase training effectiveness and value."

—**Robert O. Brinkerhoff,** Professor Emeritus, Western Michigan University; Director of Research and Evaluation, Promote International

"Navigating the complexities of measurement and evaluation for years, I find *Measurement and Evaluation on a Shoestring* to be a breath of fresh air. The 'impact hypothesis' framework elegantly simplifies the process, offering a practical lens to assess training effectiveness. It's a must-read for any L&D professional seeking to bridge the gap between program design and demonstrable results, especially when resources are limited."

—**Laurie Roth,** Learning and Development Manager, United Heritage Credit Union

"As L&D professionals, our work matters. But how do we prove it? Within these pages, Alaina provides a refreshing and highly practical guide for getting L&D programs the attention they deserve."

—**Chris Taylor,** CEO, Actionable.co

"What I appreciate most about *Measurement and Evaluation on a Shoestring* is its focus on working smarter (not harder) by being strategic, deliberate, and thoughtful. The guidance Alaina gives for how to measure results is actionable and achievable."

—**Kevin M. Yates,** L&D Detective™

"Alaina's M&E tools and resources create Cirque du Soleil–like aligned solutions that are easy to build, simple to apply, and increase training program success. This book is a must-read that cracks the code on why and how data enablement systems improve business outcomes."

—**Kathy Sebuck,** F

T0284977

On a
Shoestring
Series

Measurement and Evaluation
on a Shoestring

Alaina Szlachta, PhD

PRESS

Alexandria, VA

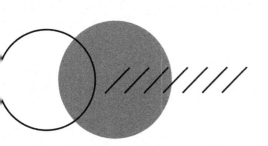

ATD Press is an internationally renowned source of insightful and practical information on talent development, training, and professional development.

ATD Press
1640 King Street
Alexandria, VA 22314 USA

Ordering information: Books published by ATD Press can be purchased by visiting ATD's website at td.org/books or by calling 800.628.2783 or 703.683.8100.

Library of Congress Control Number: 2024940207

ISBN-10: 1-95715-772-0
ISBN-13: 978-1-957157-72-6
e-ISBN: 978-1-95715-773-3

ATD Press Editorial Staff
Director: Sarah Halgas
Manager: Melissa Jones
Content Manager, Learning and Development: Jes Thompson
Developmental Editor: Jack Harlow
Production Editor: Katy Wiley Stewts
Text and Cover Designer: Shirley E.M. Raybuck

Printed by BR Printers, San Jose, CA

To the practitioners, leaders, and aspiring leaders who want to make a difference, your passion, dedication, and unwavering desire to do better motivated me to write this book.

To all the experts, theorists, researchers, and practitioners who have come before me, this book is not possible without your generous contributions to our field.

To my family and friends whose unconditional cheerleading sustains me.

Contents

ABOUT THE
ON A
SHOESTRING
SERIES

ATD's On a Shoestring series helps professionals successfully execute core topics in training and talent development when facing limitations of time, money, staff, and other resources. This series was designed for practitioners who work as a department of one, for new or "accidental" trainers, instructional designers, and learning managers who need fast, inexpensive access to practical strategies that work, and those who work for small organizations or in industries that have limited training and development resources. This book will help you whether you're new to measurement and evaluation or experienced, yet find yourself regularly limited by time, organizational support, and financial resources.

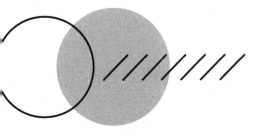

Introduction

The purpose of this book is to make measurement easier. The measurement and evaluation sector is full of incredible models, resources, and thought leaders—many of whom you'll learn more about in this book. However, these valuable assets are often underutilized—or not used at all. An interesting paradigm persists in the L&D industry. On the one hand, we all deeply desire to demonstrate the value and impact of learning in our organizations and communities. Yet, on the other hand, measurement and evaluation (M&E) are perceived as very complex, costly, time consuming, nice to have, and only quasi-essential to the L&D function. If this paradigm weren't present, M&E would be intuitively built into every learning program. Yes, measurement and evaluation can be highly complex; however, it doesn't need to be.

To break the barriers that overwhelm and intimidate most of us when we think about measurement and evaluation, we must simplify. We must find an easy starting place to integrate M&E into our L&D initiatives. Proceeding this way will build your confidence with measurement tools, establish a precedent (and I hope even excitement) to adopt M&E more regularly, and work toward improved measurement solutions in the future.

Measure What Matters— Or Why Measuring Matters

You've likely heard countless times "Measure what matters," or "What you measure improves," and "If you can't measure it, you can't manage it." This is great advice, except most of us don't know what to measure.

Consider this example: As I wrote this book, I was constantly managing my time. I needed to meet the deadline to complete this manuscript. I also needed to balance client work, business development, supporting my friends and family, and you know . . . include a little fun, rest, and relaxation. Following the recommendation of an experienced writer and editor, I used a recent writing sample to calculate roughly how many words per hour I could write. This data helped me estimate how many hours per week of writing I needed to make my deadline. With that rough words-per-hour estimate, I started blocking time on my calendar to write. I'm a big fan of having weekly goals. I love the feeling of marking "Done" next to my most important weekly action items. A few weeks into the writing process, I'd proudly marked "Done" next to the action item "Write 10 hours per week." I said to myself, "Look at me. I'm measuring my progress as I write a book on measurement!" Except there was one problem. Can you guess it? I wasn't measuring what mattered. At least, not completely.

The problem with designating 10 hours per week to write and measuring my progress toward that goal was that I was only tracking my activity. I may have sat down to write 10 hours per week, but there was no guarantee I would write any words during that time. I could succumb to writer's block, distractions, and procrastination just like everyone else.

So, what should I have been tracking instead of how much time I wrote every week? Well, the answer is not what I should be tracking *instead of* hours per week. It is what I should have been tracking *in addition to* hours per week—I also needed to be tracking the product of my activity. The product is what I did within my 10 hours of writing time. In this case, it was number of words written. Luckily, I realized my measurement mistake a few weeks into the writing process. Could you imagine if three months and 120 hours of writing time passed by before I realized that I wasn't writing as many words per hour as I originally estimated? My publisher would be very upset with me!

This simple example highlights one important dynamic in M&E. While most of us think we are measuring what matters, we are usually only measuring what is easiest. Tracking how many hours I wrote every week was relatively easy, yet it was only half of the measurement equation. I also needed to track what I did, my product, or what is commonly known as *output* in measurement speak. If my desired result was to write a 50,000-word manuscript in 12 months, the full measurement equation could look like this: First, I'd estimate my words per hour. Next, I'd start tracking my weekly activity (hours of writing) and the output of that weekly activity (words written). Finally, I'd adjust the number of hours I needed to write each week to meet the deadline based on my actual weekly output. This is measuring what matters. The magic, or the benefit behind measuring in this example, is that I can calculate accurate information about my average words per hour, which would give me a better chance of meeting my deadline. Well, so long as I also do a good job of managing writer's block, distractions, and procrastination (which are also known as *confounding variables*).

What Does It Mean to Be "On a Shoestring?"

Our struggle to measure what matters can be described in a few simple words: Lack. Of. Resources. This book is included in a series featuring information, tips, and tools to support L&D professionals "on a shoestring." Distinctly different from other topics in this series—instructional design, e-learning, and needs assessments—measurement and evaluation has historically been the underdog when it comes to resource allocation. The experience of being on a shoestring is something everyone has probably experienced at some point in their career. For many, being on a shoestring accurately describes your daily working environment. This experience means you navigate a handful of constant limitations while doing your work. Don't get me wrong; being on a shoestring is not a completely doom-and-gloom situation. Navigating limitations and still being able to do your job creates resilience, creative problem solving, and inventive thinking. As they say, the greatest innovations are born out of necessity.

What is important to know about being on a shoestring is that you aren't working with just one limitation. Instead, you're often working with overlapping limitations. If you review surveys on the state of L&D and M&E over the past 10 years—conducted by organizations such as the Association for Talent Development (ATD), Brandon Hall Group, Chief Learning Officer, Deloitte, LinkedIn Learning, LEO Learning, Watershed, Insights for Professionals, Learning Technologies Group, Mercer Mettl, and Josh Bersin—you'll notice that the reasons professionals struggle with measurement and evaluation have changed very little. Year after year, results show that lack of time, lack of support or partnership from stakeholders, limited budgets, and lack of knowledge and skills to implement measurement are key barriers to M&E. Essentially, a lack of resources.

The latest trend reports reveal six common limitations to effectively measuring and evaluating learning: constantly changing environment, feeling overwhelmed, limited leadership support, lack of knowledge and expertise, lack of resources, and limited or no budget (Figure I-1). None of these six will surprise you. As I mentioned, the struggle with M&E has been around for decades. What can be frustrating (as it surely is to me) is that the discussion often ignores the fact that these challenges are overlapping and exist simultaneously. Therefore, solutions that address one challenge at a time won't be nearly as effective as solutions that address many overlapping challenges at once.

Figure I-1. Six Common Limitations to Effectively Measuring and Evaluating Learning

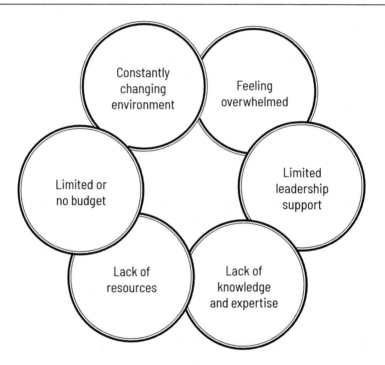

This book is written as a field guide, offering solutions to core measurement challenges and addressing the intersectional, overlapping nature of the limitations that make measurement seem just out of reach. If you've picked up this book because you are looking for simpler solutions to M&E, you feel overwhelmed by the whole idea of measurement, you are a department of one (as many L&D professionals are), or you want to expand your M&E skill set—you've found the right resource.

What Does Successful Measurement Look Like on a Shoestring?

Measurement and evaluation are processes that involve math, data, and statistics—three topics that may be your least favorite subjects. I scraped by with a C+ in high school algebra and avoided math classes as much as possible in university. Fast forward eight years, and I was teaching educational research methods to graduate students and working on a complex mixed-methods research study on culturally responsive teaching. My high school self would have laughed if she saw this in a crystal ball.

Why share this revelation? Because the elements of math, data, and statistics inherent in M&E leave most people believing that success is measured by perfection. Striving for perfection requires more time, money, and resources than we often have at our disposal. So, if we can't do it right, then why do it at all? Does this sentiment resonate with you? I always felt discouraged in my early math classes because I struggled to get answers perfectly correct—even if I understood them conceptually. Scolding from high school teachers left me thinking that math and statistics were out of reach. If a project came up that involved math or data early in my career, I would pass it off to someone I thought had more skills than I did. The reality is that I do have an objective sense for measurement and evaluation—I just needed to think about it differently. I needed to disregard perfection.

While math, data, and statistics are part of scientific processes—and yes, scientific processes require rigor, integrity, and extra degrees of thoughtfulness—they do not require perfection or even 100 percent accuracy. Scientific research inherently includes and accepts degrees of error. In fact, one of the greatest takeaways from my graduate research classes was the fact that research, measurement, and evaluation only mimic reality. Therefore, the results you get from measuring and evaluating your L&D programs will inherently feature degrees of inaccuracy. The goal is not perfection.

Success in M&E is having more information and insight than before you measured and evaluated, and having confidence that the new information has a significant degree of accuracy. With new information, you can make more informed decisions, correct course, and iterate, providing continuous improvement of your programs, processes, and procedures. With this definition of success, we don't need to be data scientists, and we can expand our thinking and skill set to identify, collect, and reflect on the most useful data, in effect, becoming stewards of continuous improvement.

Why Measurement Matters to Me

I started my career as a community-based educator in the public health sector. I initially began teaching, and then writing curriculum, followed by managing large social change programs—with government and philanthropic funders who demanded data demonstrating the programs truly made an impact. Every program development cycle began with an M&E strategy. After all, our funding and viability depended on it! Imagine my surprise when I left the public health sector after eight years to enter the corporate training arena and quickly discovered that L&D teams measured very little and rarely demonstrated the outcomes or impacts of training.

I also quickly recognized the difference between public health and corporate training program development. Public health programs compete for funding and resources. As a result, public health professionals all use a similar program development model to demonstrate anticipated outcomes and impact. The model requires a hypothesis—a chain of evidence between the education initiative and results for the target population—before receiving a green light (or funding and resources) to develop any program.

The reason for measuring education initiatives in the public health sector is to show clear and continuous improvement in public health outcomes. What, then, is the reason for measuring adult education, professional development, and training in the corporate sector? There is a clear consensus among measurement practitioners, L&D professionals, and education leaders that the purpose of M&E is twofold. First, we must show a clear and positive relationship among learning activities, skill development, and the advancement of an organization's mission and vision. Second, we have to create data that enables L&D professionals to improve their programs continuously and purposefully—creating the most timely, useful development opportunities.

While the purpose of measuring learning may be clear, most people still aren't doing it. Recent trend reports have found that only 9 percent of professionals have measurement strategies in place to show outcomes and impact, and 20 percent regularly use M&E to continuously improve their programs (Brandon Hall Group 2020). If professionals in our industry widely agree on the purpose and value of measurement and evaluation, why do we continue to struggle implementing M&E strategies?

Building M&E Strategies on a Shoestring

If your underlying goals for measurement and evaluation are to demonstrate the value of your work and be a steward of continuous improvement, how do you fulfill these goals with limited resources? Measuring and evaluating on a shoestring does not mean you have permission to cut corners, do things half-way, or sacrifice quality. Instead, we must be smarter and more strategic, seek simplification, and use the resources we have wisely. There are only so many types of resources at our disposal to pursue any project, measurement included. Using your resources—time, money, people power—wisely means making strategic choices about which resources to use to accomplish your goals. And, when resources are sparse, you must choose whether to build, borrow, or buy. It's no surprise that this book is organized around these three concepts.

Whether you work for a large enterprise, are a department of one, or create learning content for your own brand, you may always feel under-resourced when implementing an M&E strategy. Historically, organizations have not measured the outcomes and impacts of learning. Over the past 50 years, companies of all sizes have consistently been lackluster with measurement. Studies show that while many leaders desire to implement M&E, only between 9 and 35 percent of organizations (depending on the study) consistently measure the outcomes and impact of their learning programs (Brandon Hall Group 2020; ATD 2016). Even more glaring, of the organizations that reported conducting M&E, most of them only regularly measured one program. Our industry simply hasn't established a precedent of allocating resources to measurement and evaluation. Like many other learning and measurement practitioners, I sincerely hope this changes. Until then, we must get comfortable implementing measurement and evaluation on a shoestring.

The good news is that it's possible to measure and evaluate your L&D initiatives on a shoestring budget and with limited resources. However, there is one requirement: changing your thinking. In the same way I expanded my career and built confidence with research, measurement, and evaluation by letting go of perfection, this book will challenge you to change your own thinking. Historically, L&D has followed an order-taker function. Orders for training come in from leaders and we fulfill them with well-designed and delivered learning opportunities. While orders for training will continue to come in throughout your career, you must adopt a different strategy in fulfilling them.

As you've likely heard from other L&D pros, training is not always the right solution for organizational problems, despite beliefs touted by organizational leaders. To be stewards of great learning and fulfill the goals of M&E on a shoestring, we need to adopt strategies to appropriately allocate resources to the training requests received. All training programs are not equal in their scope, function, and desired outcomes. Therefore, resources for both instructional design and M&E should not be equally allocated. This book will feature strategies to help you categorize and prioritize your approach to measurement and evaluation, adopt the most appropriate measurement models and tools, and establish a precedent (and I hope excitement) to demonstrate the value of learning in your organization and community.

Build, Borrow, Buy: How to Use This Book

This book won't introduce you to a new model, framework, or theory to measure and evaluate learning. Instead, it will provide tactical guidance and measurement prescriptions that help you put into practice the core concepts, models, and theories that already exist in the field. When it comes to M&E, there is not a one-size-fits-all solution. You may be more familiar with specific measurement models over others. However, that doesn't mean those familiar models are best suited for the purpose, scope, and resources available to show the outcomes, results, impact, and insights of your unique learning initiatives. In fact, leaning on familiar models might be making measurement and evaluation more difficult than it needs to be.

Throughout this book, I share shoestring success stories featuring individuals and organizations who adopted simple strategies and thoughtful tools to demonstrate the outcomes and value of their learning programs—with very limited means. These stories feature strategies I've personally implemented throughout my career as an individual contributor, learning leader, and now educational consultant. While the current platforms, technology, and tools may change in the future, the true opportunity within each of these stories is insight into the strategic thinking associated with why and how specific tools and tactics were used.

No matter where you are currently in your career, or where your L&D work takes you in the future, there will always be times when you have limited resources, but that should never be an excuse not to implement M&E and show the outcomes and impact of your work. With limited resources you are forced to think carefully, act purposefully, and prioritize your efforts. These skills serve you no matter the size of your budget or the resources at your disposal.

While I hope you will read every chapter in this book, it's not necessary for you to sit down and read every word cover to cover. Projects, roles, and careers change constantly. I've written this book as a resource to turn to when you get "in the weeds" and need a little help from a friend (that's me) to get unstuck.

The chapters that follow are organized into three parts:

- **Build.** This part explores the fundamental components of measurement and evaluation. We'll review familiar and lesser-known measurement models and simple strategies for implementing M&E. You'll build the knowledge, perspective, and support needed to allocate your precious resources efficiently and effectively.
- **Borrow.** This part dives into methods and tactics that reduce common complexities latent in M&E and leverage novel ideas for integrating data collection into learning experience design. You'll be able to adopt time-saving strategies that borrow data you already have access to and integrate instructional and measurement design into one process.
- **Buy.** This part explores processes to help you quickly determine if buying products and hiring people to support your measurement efforts are truly worth the investment. You'll boost your confidence integrating external resources and support into your learning and measurement design strategy without breaking the bank.

In addition, don't forget to take advantage of the appendix. There you'll find more in depth measurement tools and templates (which I call "measurement prescriptions").

Let's dive in!

Recurring Elements

Throughout this book, you'll see icons marking four recurring elements:

 Time Saver: This is a strategy for shaving time off a best practice.

 On the Cheap: These are free or low-cost ideas and tools or suggestions for how to get funding.

 Deeper Dive: These are callout boxes throughout the text saying something like "Did this whet your appetite? Here's a resource to deepen your knowledge."

 Tool: This is a job aid, tool, or checklist to help you put ideas into action. You'll find tool callouts throughout the text and complete versions in the appendix.

PART I
BUILD

Working on a shoestring often means you are operating with less-than-ideal knowledge and less-than-ideal resources to evaluate program outcomes. The first part of this book provides the fundamental knowledge and best practices that are essential for you to measure and evaluate on a shoestring.

The world is full of measurement models and methods. It seems everyone on social media has a fresh tip to make evaluation easier. Books are coming out all the time with new insights to help you show your program's impact. Where should you begin? What strategies are most important for someone who has little time, resources, and knowledge but is still accountable for showing program outcomes? You'll find answers to these questions here.

In this part, you will discover how to:

- Make measurement easier by leveraging the hypothesis framework.
- Select the best M&E method for your specific program outcomes and organizational challenges.
- Understand the one thing that will help you overcome the core challenges to measuring and evaluating learning: data literacy.

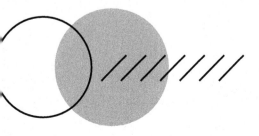

1
Simplifying Measurement With the Impact Hypothesis

Is learning the end goal, or a strategy used to achieve your end goal? If you work in K–12 or higher education, learning is often the end goal. In this sector, grade point average (GPA), capstone projects, and performance on standardized tests are commonly used as metrics to show how much students have learned. You'll rarely track how that knowledge is being applied beyond the classroom. In K–12 and higher education contexts, knowledge acquisition is the goal. You don't need to measure or evaluate anything beyond knowledge retention.

But what if you work with L&D programs for employees, customers, or consumers? Is the end goal learning, or is learning a means to an end? Learning is not the goal. In L&D programs for employees, customers, or consumers, learning is but one tool (among many) in the organizational and community development toolbox. We can use those tools to accomplish a desired result. Many professionals providing learning and development to employees, customers, or consumers have a background as either K–12 teachers, higher-education administrators, or professors. They often have little formal training in adult education. Therefore, it likely won't come as a surprise that many L&D professionals mistakenly use learning objectives (or knowledge acquisition) as the goal of their L&D initiatives. While it's important to clarify what knowledge we want people to take away from our programs, increases in knowledge are just one point at the beginning of a much larger chain of evidence showing the results, outcomes, and impact of those learning initiatives.

So, if we shouldn't be focusing solely on learning objectives, how should we think about measuring and evaluating learning? We should think like researchers and hypothesize everything!

One of the reasons measurement and evaluation can seem complex and overwhelming is that we haven't created a simple and clear picture of what exactly we are trying to accomplish—and why. Learning professionals lack an organizing framework. Now you might be thinking, "Wait. Alaina, I do have an organizing framework. I'm using Kirkpatrick's Four Levels of Evaluation or the ROI Methodology or the Learning-Transfer Evaluation Model (or whatever model you're using)." That is a fair point. Yet, in my experience, these models (and many other measurement methodologies) are much easier and more intuitive to implement when you first have a clear picture of what you are trying to do and why.

To that end, let me introduce you to (or perhaps, reacquaint you with) the hypothesis. Hypothesizing everything is the reason I find measurement and evaluation so much fun. Remember the feeling you had as a kid when someone handed you a gift to open? Remember how exciting it was not knowing what was in the beautifully wrapped package? Remember the thrill of tearing off the wrapping paper to discover what's inside? This is how I feel about measurement and evaluation. And, trust me—you can too!

To tap into the fun of measurement and evaluation (while getting the data you need to show the results and impact of your learning initiatives), you must lean into the reality that your learning programs may *not* achieve their goals. Did I just make your heart skip a beat? Good! This is the hard reality that we face—and why M&E is such an important part of our work. Even with the most thoughtfully designed programs, there is no guarantee our L&D initiatives will generate the intended outcomes. It's just a hypothesis. A hope. A dream. An aspiration.

This is where the fun comes in! We get to be researchers when we measure and evaluate. We get to discover new insights, uncover untold stories, and equip ourselves with information to improve our work. Yet, before all that becomes possible, you must begin with an impact hypothesis, which is your organizing framework. It is the story you hope to tell when your program is over.

TIME SAVER
The Differences Between Measurement, Evaluation, Assessment, and Research

A question I get asked a lot when I facilitate training programs and workshops is, "What is the difference between measurement, evaluation, assessment, and research?" The answer is especially important for professionals working on a shoe-string, who often feel overwhelmed by the idea of measuring and evaluating learning. Being able to define these terms and their corresponding function is incredibly helpful as you build your M&E skill set. Here's how you can think of these four terms:

- **Measurement** is the act of collecting and analyzing data to calculate relationships among key variables involved in evaluating your L&D initiatives.
- **Evaluation** is a process that, when executed, tells you whether you achieved your L&D initiative's goals.
- **Assessment** is a tool that provides data you can use to measure relationships among key variables. You can use assessment tools that have been created by industry leaders, such as the Clifton Strengths Finder, the Intercultural Development Inventory, or the DISC personality assessment. You can also create your own assessments, such as a survey or exam. In some instances, an assessment is simply one question that gives you qualitative or quantitative data to support your measurement needs.
- **Research** is a process undertaken to show statistically significant outcomes, which are then featured in peer-reviewed journals, clinical trials, and longitudinal studies to help others make important decisions, such as in public health or other government policies.

When measuring and evaluating learning, you can use similar thinking, strategies, and tactics as researchers. However, your goals will rarely be the same as a researcher's. Most importantly, the level of rigor used in research methods is not the same as measuring the results of L&D initiatives. In M&E, it is perfectly fine to strive for correlations instead of causation. Keeping it simple is often the best course of action. Complexity can always be added later. If you believe complex and rigorous methods are the best M&E tactics, you may never be comfortable doing any M&E work at all.

Starting With an Impact Hypothesis to Get Stakeholder Buy-In

I'd like to tell you a story about how thinking like a researcher and hypothesizing everything not only made measurement easier for Chase Damiano—a leadership development professional who has always been passionate about showing how investments in leadership create a measurable impact—it also provided insights to get stakeholder buy-in, improve the learning experience, and expand results for future learners.

Chase was struggling to get buy-in from stakeholders to design and deliver a leadership development program focused on building delegation skills. He often heard anecdotally from newly promoted managers that they were working long hours. They found themselves doing the same work from their previous role in addition to new leadership activities. Some of these new managers even said they were so stressed they wanted to quit.

After hearing numerous compelling anecdotes, Chase's stakeholders agreed to test the leadership program with a small pilot group. Before the leadership program could be embedded into the new manager onboarding, Chase needed to show that delegation was an essential skill to help new managers work fewer hours, reduce stress, and be more optimistic about their new position. Chase was ecstatic to get permission to move forward, yet when he thought about showing that improved delegation skills would reduce working hours, reduce stress, and improve optimism, he felt defeated. "Where do I begin?" he wondered. "How will I prove this training works with no additional resources to measure and evaluate?"

Chase had a loose hypothesis: New managers were overworking, experiencing higher levels of stress, and had a negative outlook about their managerial role. Chase thought these outcomes were related to managers holding on to too many individual contributor tasks from their former role while also taking on activities in their new leadership role. After talking with a few recently promoted managers, he thought that teaching them how to delegate would solve their pain points.

This was a great start. The next step was to use an organizing framework (a hypothesis) to clarify what Chase wanted to do and why. By formalizing his hypothesis, he could figure out how to evaluate the pilot leadership program and show stakeholders the results they wanted to see. Essentially, he could determine what data he needed to collect to prove whether his hypothesis was correct. Here's where I could help.

On a whiteboard I wrote down, "If X, then Y." This formula is something I started incorporating into my practice after reading about it in John Boulmetis and Phyllis Dutwin's 2011 book *The ABCs of Evaluation*. It's the first step to creating an evaluation strategy.

X and Y are the first two points in the chain of evidence necessary to prove a hypothesis. For Chase, X was his leadership program, while Y represented the change in knowledge, skills, and mindset (or attitude) he wanted the leadership program to influence.

So, for Chase's leadership program, the statement would read, "If X (managers complete the leadership development program), then Y (they will improve their delegation skills). See Figure 1-1 for a visual.

Figure 1-1. The First Link in the Chain of Evidence

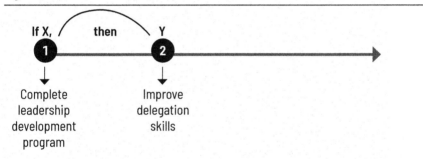

But Chase had to continue one step further: "If X, then Y, then Z." Z is the "so what" part of the hypothesis, as in, if employees increase their delegation skills, then so what? Z represents the immediate outcomes Chase expected to see if managers were better at delegation.

In the short-term (immediately after increasing their delegation skills), Chase thought that managers would work fewer hours per week, be less stressed, and be more optimistic about their role. This was the short-term answer to the question, "So what?" (Z_s). However, there is one final point in the chain of evidence—a long-term answer to the question, "So what?" (Z_L). So, "If Z_s, then Z_L."

After some thought about the longer-term outcomes of new managers working less and being less stressed and more optimistic, Chase posited that new managers would spend more time working on strategic leadership activities and less time on individual contributor tasks. As a result, they would be more likely to stay in their role longer than if they hadn't improved their ability to delegate.

Now, Chase could complete the organizing framework showing what the leadership program was designed to do—and why (Figure 1-2).

Figure 1-2. Completing the Chain of Evidence

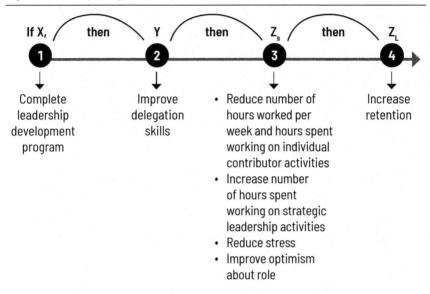

This organizing framework was the strategy Chase needed to show stakeholders the importance of delegation skills in the overall approach to onboarding and retaining new managers.

With a clear hypothesis in place, his next step was to prove it. I'll tell you how Chase's story turned out at the end of this chapter, but before that, let's explore how you can apply the hypothesis framework to your L&D initiatives.

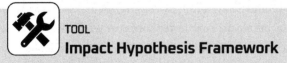

TOOL
Impact Hypothesis Framework

The appendix includes a blank hypothesis framework that you can use.

Applying the Impact Hypothesis to Your L&D Initiatives

I know what you may be thinking. No one in a corporate learning environment will be given the green light to use precious time to prove a hypothesis before developing a training program. I agree with you. Corporate working environments move very quickly, and not everyone has the time to consistently do pilot testing like Chase did and like I've done in the public health sector. You can, however, use the hypothesis framework to organize your thinking. Then, you can show how learning programs are intended to inform and change skills and attitudes, and link those changes to short-term and long-term outcomes. Even better, you can leverage these hypotheses in several ways to not only improve each individual program, but to adapt your overall learning strategy.

When I speak at conferences and facilitate workshops to help L&D professionals build their M&E skills, I often hear people say:

> "Measurement and evaluation is so time consuming. As soon as we get our measurement systems up and running, something changes and the program we are evaluating is no longer a priority. We know M&E is important, yet how are we supposed to show the outcomes of our programs when the organization's priorities are constantly changing?"

Does this resonate with you? My own research, and research done by other M&E professionals such as Robert Brinkerhoff, reveals that having a complementary and supportive environment determines 80 percent of a learning initiative's success (Mooney and Brinkerhoff 2008). Quality content does not determine success; it's important, but to a lesser degree than you may think. Learner satisfaction also does not determine success. Instead, success depends on how well your organization's working environment supports and reinforces new skills learned in training—and learners agree! According to a 2024 report from TalentLMS and Vyond on what employees want in their workplace learning experience, 80 percent of employees said personalization was important to them.

Personalization means designing learning opportunities to meet learners where they are literally (their workplace environment) and experientially (accounting for their experience level and existing skill set). Environment also has a significant influence on the success of your M&E strategies. If your working environment and organization's priorities are constantly changing, your M&E strategies may suffer, or worse, be a waste of time and resources. This is a reality you will likely never escape because the world is changing at an incredibly fast pace. For businesses to remain viable, they must also change and adapt. Therefore, you must be agile with your L&D and M&E strategies. What is the one thing you can do to be agile with measurement and evaluation? Hypothesize everything!

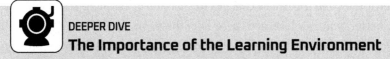

DEEPER DIVE
The Importance of the Learning Environment

For more information, check out the 2008 book *Courageous Training* by Tim Mooney and Robert O. Brinkerhoff. Read chapter 9, "Diary of a CLO," to learn how Children's Healthcare of Atlanta, Georgia, discovered that having the right environment was one of the most significant contributors to their program's success.

Using Hypotheses to Be Agile in a Changing Work Environment

Imagine it's Monday morning. You're sitting in a conference room with your team ready for the weekly kick-off meeting. In walks your boss, who says, "Well team, we must make another pivot. Our stakeholders want to launch a new affiliate partnership program. The goals are to improve our visibility in the marketplace, improve customer retention, and increase conversion rates with prospective customers. What learning initiatives do we currently have that are designed to influence these key performance indicators (KPIs)? We want to integrate the new affiliate partnership strategy into the programs we're currently running."

If you were sitting in that meeting, what would you do to find all the current learning programs designed to increase those specific KPIs? How difficult would it be for you, your team, or your team leader? Perhaps you already have systems in place to identify which learning initiatives are designed to influence current KPIs. If so, congratulations! You are on the right track. However, if you are among the many learning professionals working on a shoestring—with limited resources and less than ideal experience with measurement and evaluation—you may have no idea how to answer this question. That's OK too. You're in good company.

Hypothesizing everything is the solution. And it's easier than you might think.

Let's return to the Monday morning meeting. Your boss asks, "What learning initiatives do we currently have that are designed to influence these KPIs?" In response, you could say, "Let me take a look at our learning strategy tracker" (Table 1-1).

Table 1-1. A Learning Strategy Tracker

Status	Program Name	Target Audience	KSA Goal	Short-Term Goal	Long-Term Goal
Active	New Sales Leader Onboarding	Newly hired sales leaders	Demonstrate 80% or higher competency practicing the sales closing process	Close 15% of sales calls within their first 90 days	100% of new sales team members achieve a 90-day time to value

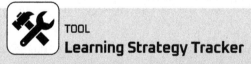

TOOL
Learning Strategy Tracker

The appendix includes a blank template you can use as inspiration for your learning strategy tracker, although, you'll want to digitize it for easy searchability.

Your learning strategy tracker spreadsheet ideally includes every one of your active, currently in development, and recently completed learning initiatives for the year. You should also record these data points for each program:

- **Target audience**—the people you're developing the initiative for
- **KSA goals**—the targeted changes in knowledge, skills, and attitudes

- **Short-term goals**—the targeted changes in performance your training program (if successful) should immediately influence
- **Long-term goals**—the targeted changes in the business's strategic KPIs

In the Monday morning meeting example, you could sort the data by the short-term outcomes column and search for the relevant performance-specific KPIs, such as resolving customer complaint calls within three minutes, achieving a 100 percent accuracy rate with new client intake interactions, or decreasing error rates to 25 percent or lower. Or, you could sort the data by long-term strategic business KPIs, such as improving employee or customer retention, increasing revenue, or expanding market share.

Then, you can tell your boss, "I see there are three programs we can adapt right away: New Sales Leader Onboarding, New Sales Team Onboarding, and the Monthly Sales Enablement Series. These programs target our entire sales team (new and tenured, leadership, and individual contributors). Who else needs to know about this new affiliate partnership program? What is the best way to train them or communicate these updates?"

That entire interaction could take less than 60 seconds, and it's all made possible by a simple organizing framework—the hypothesis.

Another great reason for creating a hypothesis for every learning program, and housing that information in a learning strategy tracker, is adapting to changing priorities. Here is a common scenario: Yesterday, three KPIs were the driving force of your business. Today, those three KPIs have been replaced by something else. What do you do with the learning strategy and programs you built around yesterday's KPIs?

The *2022 Workplace Learning Trends Report* from TalentLMS and the Society for Human Resource Management (SHRM) found two common barriers to training effectiveness: outdated programs and irrelevant content. You can imagine how changing priorities play a role in these barriers.

It can be difficult to respond appropriately to change if you don't have a clear picture of what you're doing and why. Creating a hypothesis for every learning program and storing that information in an easily accessible location (like a collaborative digital spreadsheet) gives you the ability to be agile when facing change. Your learning strategy tracker becomes a prioritization tool. When priorities change, you can search for learning programs designed to influence deprioritized KPIs, and then ask yourself:

- Are these programs still relevant?
- How do you adapt your current and future learning opportunities to meet new priorities?

When stakeholders ask you to create new learning programs, you can ask them these questions as part of your training request intake process:

- What KPIs do you want this program to influence?
- If you're unsure what KPIs this program should influence, who can you talk to for clarity on the program's intended performance and strategic business goals before moving forward?
- My team is currently at capacity and prioritizing [insert specific] programs that are designed to influence [insert specific] outcomes. Which program would you like us to deprioritize so we can take on this new request?
- Before building a new program, can I explore what programs are already designed to influence those KPIs and decide whether a new program is necessary?

The L&D function has historically been an underused organization development asset. Doing great work often requires that we swim upstream—constantly navigating floating debris, hidden rocks, and other obstacles. The most undesirable circumstance is an unsupportive organizational environment. Current and historical trends indicate this is unlikely to change. In a 2022 Mercer Mettl study, 38 percent of learning leaders said, "The absence of a structured organizational focus and strategy" is the greatest challenge to doing great L&D work. Meanwhile, 41 percent of L&D professionals cited competing organizational priorities as the reason they weren't measuring or evaluating learning (Lea and Ells 2022). Another 2023 trend report from LinkedIn Learning found that only half of learning professionals worked closely with executive leaders as they developed learning initiatives. Finally, the most depressing trend of all is that 50 percent of HR leaders reported that measuring and evaluating learning was not a top priority for their stakeholders (Insights for Professionals 2023).

I don't think any of these statistics will come as a surprise to you. If you've been working in the L&D function as long as I have—or perhaps even longer—this is likely your reality. So, if you're looking to collaborate more with stakeholders and encourage them prioritize M&E, a hypothesis for every learning program creates a compelling starting place to build those strategic partnerships.

I hope this inspires you to go forth and create a hypothesis for each of your learning initiatives and build a learning strategy tracker immediately. Change, clarity, and improved results await you once you've completed this project!

Brainstorming Possible Metrics by Creating a Hypothesis

True or false? All data is good data. You've probably heard the saying, "garbage in, garbage out." This means if you are working with bad data, you'll also end up with bad results. So, is all data good? No. A common challenge among learning professionals is determining the most appropriate metrics to evaluate learning. The most common metrics used in the industry are learner satisfaction rate, program completion rate, net promoter score, and knowledge increases. These metrics may be common, but that doesn't mean they are the best for evaluating learning. In fact, they tell you absolutely nothing about skill development, performance improvement, or application of new knowledge on the job.

The most appropriate metrics are the ones that tell you whether the learning program influenced progress in the way you desired. What can you do to find these metrics? Create a hypothesis.

Let's return to Chase. Once he created his hypothesis (that new managers who practice delegation are going to feel more optimistic about their work, work less hours, and stay longer in their role), he needed to prove it. He needed to choose the best data to test his hypothesis.

Chase planned to assess changes in managers' delegation practices using simulations and projects and created a rubric to evaluate performance growth. He asked them at four key points before, during, and after the program to rate their level of stress, how many hours they work every week, and how likely they were to stay in their new role. This gave him an outline of the metrics to evaluate his programs' effectiveness, which were:

- Delegation practices
- Optimism
- Weekly hours worked
- Likelihood of staying in the manager role

These metrics also happen to be listed in his hypothesis statement under the short- and long-term outcomes. In many cases, your short- and long-term outcomes may also be the direct metrics you'll use to evaluate your program, but not always. To determine if your short- and long-term outcomes can also be your metrics, ask yourself, "How do I measure that?"

For Chase, his first short-term outcome was to reduce the number of working hours per week. He could measure that by asking people to look at their calendars and calculate the approximate number of hours worked in the past week. Determining how to measure the change in number of hours worked each week and the percentage of time worked in leadership versus on individual contributor activities is easy because employees can look at their calendars (a tangible asset) to formulate an accurate answer. However, what if you want to measure something less tangible, like improved relationships?

Another short-term outcome might be for new managers to build stronger relationships with their direct reports. There are many ways to measure that. In this example, strong relationships are an outcome and not a metric. To get to an appropriate metric, Chase would need to dig deeper by asking a follow up question, such as, "What are the indicators that relationships between managers and direct reports are strong?" From that list, Chase could select one or more metrics that are best suited for his context.

Chase's story shows, yet again, the power of a hypothesis. Whether or not the outcomes are the metrics to evaluate your learning program—you still look to the outcomes as the first step in determining your metrics. And, you wouldn't have any clear outcomes without a complete hypothesis.

Follow these steps to translate your outcomes into metrics:

1. List your short- and long-term outcomes.
2. For each outcome, ask yourself, "How do I measure that?"
3. If you can easily come up with a way to realistically measure the outcome, then the outcome is a metric.
4. If you don't know how to measure the outcome, or if there are many ways to measure it, then your outcome is an outcome. In this case, you must dig deeper to find appropriate metrics. Ask yourself, "What are the indicators that (the outcome) is present?"
5. For each item on your list of indicators, ask yourself, "How do I measure that?"
6. Once you can easily come up with a realistic measurement solution, you'll have arrived at your metrics.

So, why is Chase's case study an example of a shoestring success story? Using the hypothesis framework saved him time when developing the new manager training program and evaluating its effectiveness. Chase was able to add what he thought would be a game changing development opportunity for new managers at his company. To get buy-in from stakeholders he had only one shot to show the program's impact.

Going into this project with a clear hypothesis of what he was doing and why kept him focused. Remember, Chase hadn't yet developed the new manager training program. He not only had to design and deliver the pilot program, he also had to evaluate it. Thanks to his clear hypothesis that practicing delegation skills would lead to reduced time spent on individual contributor activities and increased time spent on manager-level activities, Chase was able to design his learning experience around those core concepts. New training programs often include too much information, and it takes time to refine them to the optimal ratio of information, practice, and social learning. Chase didn't have time to waste, so he centered the information, practice, and social learning around how to delegate individual contributor activities.

In the end, Chase's pilot program demonstrated that participants who completed the practice activities with an average or above performance score saw the highest increases in time spent on manager-level activities and largest decreases on time spent on individual contributor activities. While data from the pilot evaluation did not prove that new managers reduced the number of hours working each week, it did show that they felt more optimistic in their roles overall. Chase's delegation training program is now offered on a quarterly basis to new managers at his company.

A Shoestring Summary

The most important thing we can do to measure and evaluate program outcomes on a shoestring is to start somewhere that is exciting and accessible. While each item in this shoestring chapter summary is useful and will improve your ability to capture program outcomes, results, or impact, doing everything on this list may seem overwhelming. If you can only do one thing, start with number 1, and add more complexity later.

1. **Create a hypothesis.** In this chapter, I encouraged you to hypothesize everything. That may be your end goal, but it is surely not your

starting place. Instead, I suggest you hypothesize *something*. Pick one learning initiative, a new or old one. Use the hypothesis to clarify what you are doing and why and create your measurement strategy. You could create a hypothesis for one of your flagship learning programs (often a leadership development program or onboarding program) to help validate and solidify what you are doing and why. Perhaps you can create or refine the existing evaluation strategy for your flagship program. Start somewhere. Start with one hypothesis.

2. **Share the hypothesis framework with your L&D team.** Once you've made a loose hypothesis for the learning initiative, share it with your team. If you have an example hypothesis in hand, it is easier to share the value of the hypothesis framework. Ideally you could enroll other members of your team to adopt this framework and create hypotheses for other important learning initiatives.

3. **Create a learning strategy tracker.** Maybe you only have one or two initiatives listed. This is a great starting place. Add more initiatives as time or team-member support allows.

4. **Share the learning strategy tracker with your L&D team.** This resource is useless if it's not adopted by your entire department. The learning strategy tracker gives all members of your team equal visibility into what you are doing and why for every learning initiative. Your team can be more agile, and you'll ultimately be better able to support your business through learning.

5. **Brainstorm your metrics.** Your goal is to have one to three metrics for each outcome. More is not always better! Keep it simple.

2

Aligning Your Measurement Strategy: Models and Tactics

Let's start off with a quick quiz. Review this list of models and theories and make a physical or mental check mark by all the models you are familiar with:

- ❏ Action Mapping
- ❏ Anderson's Value of Learning Model
- ❏ Balanced Scorecard
- ❏ Brinkerhoff's Success Case Method (SCM)
- ❏ Context Input Process Product (CIPP) Model
- ❏ Context Input Reaction Output (CIRO) Model
- ❏ Discrepancy Evaluation Model (DEM)
- ❏ Gilbert's Behavior Engineering Model (BEM)
- ❏ Goal-Free Evaluation
- ❏ Kirkpatrick's Four Levels of Evaluation
- ❏ Learning-Transfer Evaluation Model (LTEM)
- ❏ Measurement Map
- ❏ Return on Expectations (ROE) Methodology
- ❏ ROI Methodology
- ❏ Talent Development Reporting Principles (TDRp) Framework

How many of these models do you know? Would you be surprised if I told you this is just a small fraction of all the models and methods currently available to help you evaluate learning? After reviewing the literature dating back to

1930, I found approximately 40 models across multiple professional disciplines—all designed to help measure and evaluate adult education. I'm sure I've missed many models, and more will be developed as new practitioners rise in the field.

What does this tell us about our approach to measuring and evaluating learning? Having done M&E work in a few different sectors (government, non-profit, higher education, and corporate learning), I was aware of many available models to guide an M&E approach. But, as I kept adding new ones to the list, my initial reaction was, "Wow! How could I not know about these amazing frameworks?" There are three primary reasons I suspect we aren't familiar many of these models:

- **Lack of access to academic research.** When you leave undergraduate or graduate academic institutions, your access to physical and digital research goes away too. And people who didn't attend college or university likely never had access to these resources in the first place. On a positive note, I began using my local library again while writing this book. I was able to access many resources (including physical books, e-books, and academic research articles) for free just by renewing my library card.

- **Inequitable marketing.** Some of these models have been turned into large business ventures, while others were published one or two times and never marketed at all. In many cases, the information you can easily access (especially online) via conferences or continuing education is determined by the size of the marketing budget. It's not that this information is bad; it's simply painting an incomplete picture of all the information and resources available on measurement and evaluation.

- **The historical practice of disciplinary silos.** HR, higher education, corporate learning, public health, adult education, social work, and so on—each of these disciplines has at least one model (if not significantly more) to guide practitioners in measuring and evaluating the inputs, activities, outputs, outcomes, results, and impact of their work. Silos and fragmentation were originally created for simplification and efficiency. Now, these same silos are leading to duplicated work, blind spots, and limited collaboration (among other things). There is much to be learned by stepping outside your discipline. You can often find answers to questions and fresh perspectives in unexpected places.

This leads to a relevant follow-up question: Are you using the best models, theories, and tools for your evaluation needs?

TIME SAVER
Consensus App

While writing this book, I discovered Consensus, which is a new tool that uses AI to synthesize more than 200 million peer-reviewed papers and scientific journal articles. It allows anyone to search for free to find data, insights, frameworks, and theories on nearly any topic. Explore more at consensus.app.

This book is written for professionals working on a shoestring—L&D professionals with limited time, resources, and support. Two consistently reported obstacles to measuring and evaluating learning are time and money. What if the measurement models you are most familiar with are also the ones that require more of these precious resources? What if there are more appropriate models that also cost less?

If there is only one message you take from this book, I hope it's this: You may be using the wrong model to measure and evaluate learning. Is the M&E process costly and time consuming? Or is it the model you are using to measure and evaluate learning?

Let's pause for a moment. What I've just suggested is a perspective that I hope has fired up your neurons, sparking some cognitive dissonance. Pushing the boundaries of your knowledge comfort zone is this first step to expanding your thinking and broadening your skill sets. To help you find the measurement model best suited for your evaluation needs, I'd like to share another shoestring success story.

Find Your Measurement Model Fit and Save Resources

Sarah and Jordan are co-founders of an improv-centered leadership development company. Their signature program was a 90-minute workshop introducing leaders to improv as a tool for fostering collaboration, trust, and connection among teams. However, Sarah and Jordan wanted to expand the workshop into a more in-depth experiential learning opportunity and sell it to corporate clients. Before they could do this, they needed a solid business case demonstrating the value of improv as a leadership development tool.

As a start-up business, they had little budget to invest in a robust study to explore the ROI of their improv-centered leadership training. Limited time was also a factor. The sooner they could put together a business case, the sooner they could bring in revenue through training program sales. They also weren't overly familiar with M&E methods. A true shoestring scenario.

Sarah and Jordan both had corporate backgrounds and knew that business leaders would likely only take their improv leadership training seriously if there was a compelling return on investment. Therefore, they thought leaning into the ROI Methodology was the best course of action.

They asked me to help them implement a measurement solution. We began by creating a hypothesis about how improv develops better leaders. They soon landed on this one: "Applying common practices from improv can foster innovation, optimism, and a sense of psychological safety among team members; the improv mindset can help leaders respond better to change." Armed with a clear hypothesis, they needed to find or collect data to show how improv skills and an improv mindset can influence the outcomes of innovation, optimism, psychological safety and change management. Fortunately, Jordan knew of research showing the links between active listening, collaboration, innovation, optimism (all skills fostered by practicing improv) and leaders' ability to create psychologically safe environments. I also knew of research correlating organizations with psychologically safe workplaces and higher levels of retention and productivity.

Ultimately, Sarah and Jordan didn't need an ROI calculation—recent research had done the ROI investigation for them by showing that improving psychological safety in the workplace leads to higher retention and productivity. They simply needed to show a strong relationship between leaders' growth in improv skills and their ability to foster psychological safety. Instead of ROI, they needed a different model—the Measurement Map, a model that links employees' actions and behaviors with key business performance indicators (which we'll get to later in this chapter).

Applying a Measurement Model to Your L&D Initiatives

What is the purpose of a measurement and evaluation model? It is a guide suggesting appropriate steps to help you accomplish your evaluation goals. One common misperception about measurement models is that they can prescribe your goals or intended outcomes. There are models and theories available to help you identify the goals and possible results of a learning program. However, those would not be M&E models. Only after your goals are known, and ideally agreed upon by stakeholders, can M&E models be effective.

The way most learning professionals approach selecting an M&E model is by searching, "measurement and evaluation models" online, coming up with a list of models, and picking the one that makes the most sense for their needs. This strategy to finding a model fit isn't all bad; you need to select a model that makes the most sense for your needs. However, the model you choose can be the difference between creating an effective measurement strategy and wasting time and resources.

So, how do you select the right model for your M&E needs? Let's explore your options.

The Difference Between M&E Strategy and Tactics

I'll never forget the first time someone asked me to describe the difference between strategy and tactics. It was in a workshop focused on creating effective goals. I stared back at the instructor with a baffled look and no coherent answer came to mind. I knew they were different, but I was simply unable to articulate how. The difference between strategy and tactics is what distinguishes an M&E strategy from the models used to measure and evaluate learning. If you're thinking, "Wait! Isn't the M&E model my M&E strategy?" The answer is no.

Selecting an M&E model is not the same as creating an M&E strategy. Your M&E strategy outlines at a high level what you are doing and why, and helps you identify possible data needed to demonstrate if you are effective. Measurement models don't determine the high-level goals of your learning programs or their intended outcomes. This is why the hypothesis framework (which I outlined in chapter 1) is so helpful. M&E models can help you refine your strategy; however, their greatest function is to provide tactics, steps, action plans, and detailed how-tos for calculating the relationship between the inputs, outputs, activities, outcomes, results, and impact of your L&D work.

All M&E work boils down to these two components:

- **Measurement and evaluation strategy.** This is the story you want to tell describing the results and impact of your learning program. Use the hypothesis framework to organize your story to show the high-level domino effect the learning program will have on knowledge, skills, and abilities (KSA) and short- and long-term outcomes.
- **Measurement and evaluation tactics.** These are the steps taken to calculate the relationship among the inputs, activities, outputs, outcomes, impacts, and results. All M&E models use some or all of the elements listed in Table 2-1 (Dolfing 2020).

Table 2-1. Core Elements of Measurement and Evaluation Models

Element	Definition	Example Metrics	Example Results
Inputs	Resources used to bring the learning program to life	• Time of internal or external employees to design and deliver the program • Finances in the form of money, hardware, or software • Office space to host in-person learning events	• Build the program by a specific deadline. • Build the program within a specific number of hours. • Build the program at or under budget.
Activities	What people do to achieve the goals of the program	• Amount of time learners are allotted to participate in the program	• Participants complete the program in the time allotted to complete the activities.
Outputs	Direct, immediate-term results associated with a learning program	• Completion rates of core program features (such as videos, case studies, quizzes, and discussion boards)	• Participants complete 80 percent of key program features.

Table 2-1. (cont.)

Element	Definition	Example Metrics	Example Results
Outcomes	Medium-term consequences of the program that are measured after the program has been implemented and over a defined period of time (Outcomes for learning programs are always performance related)	• Percent of policies being accurately followed • Decreased errors of data inputs • Increased adherence to customer complaint practices • Increased opportunities to lower operational costs • Improved team dynamics	• Comparison of baseline and post-program data shows progress toward the targeted outcomes.
Impacts	The long-term consequences of a program (These are possible because of a change in performance outcomes)	• What becomes possible over time when the performance outcomes are continuously maintained	• Compare projected versus actual impact (based on the achievement of activities, outputs, and outcomes).
Results	A reflection of the data from outputs, outcomes, and impacts used to determine the overall success of the program (Were the targets for all core elements met?)	• Gap between goals and targets for each element of the program	• Success in one does not guarantee success in another. However, success rates—or lack thereof—provide insights into where to focus energy to improve future program results.

To summarize the difference between strategy and tactics when measuring and evaluating learning, consider this: The *M&E strategy* is your big vision, ideally drawn physically or digitally in a storyboard, showing the intended results of your learning program. *M&E tactics* are the specific actions you take to collect the right data and then calculate relationships among the core elements (inputs, activities, outputs, outcomes, impacts, and results). Use the hypothesis framework to craft your big vision (or strategy). Select one or more M&E models to create tactics to calculate the results of your learning program.

Using Storyboarding to Outline Your M&E Strategy

Consider the process of measuring and evaluating learning like a puzzle. Imagine the puzzle pieces are scattered on a table, and you are trying to figure out how they fit together, while also looking out for any missing pieces. Returning to Sarah and Jordan's story, they used the hypothesis framework to reveal all the puzzle pieces necessary to create a business case for their improv training and transferred them into a storyboard to work out their data collection strategy.

TIME SAVER
Storyboarding

Storyboards can look many different ways. Perhaps you or your team have a storyboard format you already use during the instructional design process. That's great! Storyboarding is also a powerful tool for outlining your M&E strategy. If storyboarding is new to you, or you've never used a storyboard specifically for M&E, pay special attention to how the pieces of Sarah and Jordan's puzzle come together one step at a time, so you can use their experience as an example for how to storyboard your hypothesis framework to find the missing pieces and weak links within your M&E strategy.

To find all the pieces of your M&E puzzle, you need to answer the question, "What's your hypothesis for how *the focus of the training* develops *your target audience*?" Let's use Sarah and Jordan's example as a guide. They wanted to explore how *improv practices* could develop *leaders*. They thought leaders (their target audience) who practiced improv (the focus of their training) would experience the following outcomes:

- Improved optimism and innovation for the individual leader
- Improved innovation for the individual leader

- Increased collaboration among teams
- Increased psychological safety in the working environment
- Increased retention
- Increased productivity

Imagine the outcomes are all separate puzzle pieces. With your pieces laid out, you can then return to your hypothesis framework and start putting the puzzle together. Remember, the goal of the hypothesis framework is to understand what you're doing and why by linking together four key puzzle pieces—the development opportunity, changes in KSAs, and short- and long-term outcomes (Figure 2-1). Identifying the possible variables in your impact hypothesis is the first step toward creating your data collection strategy.

Figure 2-1. The Impact Hypothesis Framework

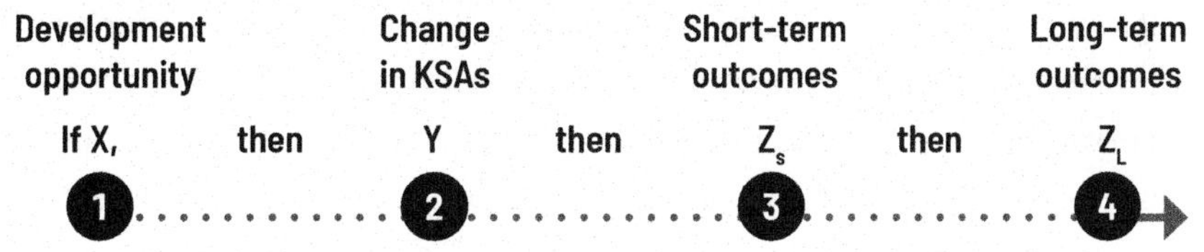

Development opportunity		Change in KSAs		Short-term outcomes		Long-term outcomes
If X,	then	Y	then	Z_s	then	Z_L
1	....	2	....	3	....	4 →

In Figure 2-1, you'll see a dotted line between the four puzzle pieces (or variables). The next step is figuring out what data is needed to explore the relationship between each variable. Until you have enough data to prove there is a strong relationship between each variable, those lines will remain dotted (indicating an uncertain or weak link between the variables). Your goal is to demonstrate strong relationships (solid lines) between all variables.

Let's continue storyboarding Sarah and Jordan's big vision to look for weak links between the puzzle pieces.

Figure 2-2 shows how the four key pieces of Sarah and Jordan's measurement puzzle fit into the hypothesis framework. With their impact hypothesis in place, they were ready to put it to the test by collecting their own data (primary sources) and leveraging evidence from other people's studies (secondary sources) to create strong relationships (solid lines) between each puzzle piece.

Figure 2-2. Sarah and Jordan's Impact Hypothesis

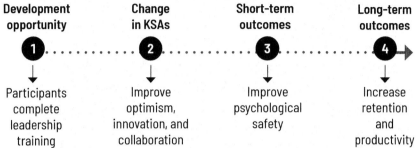

Development opportunity	Change in KSAs	Short-term outcomes	Long-term outcomes
Participants complete leadership training	Improve optimism, innovation, and collaboration	Improve psychological safety	Increase retention and productivity

DEEPER DIVE

Needs Assessment

If it was difficult for you to answer the question, "What's your hypothesis for how the focus of your training develops your target audience?" you'll need to do some prework in the form of a needs assessment. The hypothesis framework is just an organizing tool, setting you up for success to collect the right data to show strong relationships among a series of variables. The hypothesis framework can help you clarify and better articulate what those variables are. However, for the hypothesis framework to be useful, you must have a general idea of what those variables are to begin with.

To identify those variables, conduct a needs assessment. And, lucky for you, I have the perfect recommendation. Check out another book in this series, *Needs Assessment on a Shoestring* by Kelly L. Jones and Jody N. Lumsden (2023). Also, in the appendix, you'll find a list of essential questions from their book that you can use to discover the most important gaps your learning solution should address when you have limited time for an in-depth analysis.

Jordan knew of many peer-reviewed journal articles demonstrating strong correlations between psychologically safe workplaces (their short-term outcome) and increased retention and productivity (their long-term outcomes). Thus, we could replace the dotted line with a solid line to indicate reliable data establishing a strong relationship between psychologically safe workplaces and retention and productivity (Figure 2-3).

Figure 2-3. Storyboarding a Strong Relationship Between Variables 3 and 4

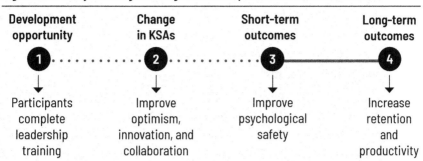

Sarah also had access to a few informal studies demonstrating a positive relationship between optimism, innovative thinking, and collaborative teams and feelings of psychologically safety in the workplace. Evidence from Sarah's studies created a semi-strong link between variable 2 (changes in KSAs) and variable 3 (short-term outcomes), which is represented by the gray semi-solid line in Figure 2-4. They strengthened this link by collecting their own (primary) data. (We'll dive into how they collected data later in this chapter.)

Figure 2-4. Storyboarding a Semi-Strong Relationship Between Variables 2 and 3

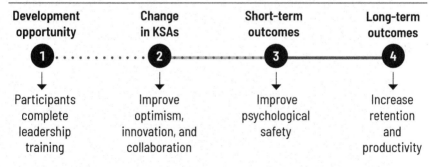

Now that we've officially put together all the pieces of Sarah and Jordan's M&E puzzle, the storyboarding work is complete. Remember, the goal of drawing out the hypothesis of a learning program's intended impact is to find the missing pieces of the M&E strategy. The complete storyboard in Figure 2-4 shows the two missing pieces of Sarah and Jordan's M&E strategy:

1. They don't have any data showing a relationship between their improv-centered leadership development program and changes in the following KSAs:
   ◦ Innovation and collaboration (skills and practices)
   ◦ Optimism (attitude)
2. They don't have enough data to prove the relationship between changes in innovation, collaboration, and optimism with increased feelings of psychological safety in the participant's team or workplace.

The dotted line, semi-solid gray line, and solid black line linking Sarah and Jordan's puzzle pieces show how to focus the data collection (and analysis) efforts (Table 2-2).

Table 2-2. Turning Observations Into Action Using Sarah and Jordan's Measurement Puzzle

Observation	Significance	Action
Dotted line between variables 1 and 2	Weak link between the development opportunity and KSA changes	Find an M&E model prescribing tactics for evaluating changes in KSAs.
Semi-solid gray line between variables 2 and 3	Semi-strong link between KSA changes and short-term outcomes	Find an M&E model or create tactics that provide data to show the relationship between KSA changes and short-term outcomes.
Solid black line between variables 3 and 4	Strong link between short- and long-term outcomes	No measurement action is necessary. Record the key data points from existing research to demonstrate the strong relationship between short- and long-term outcomes.

In chapter 1, I mentioned that more data is not necessarily better. This is especially true if you are a professional working on a shoestring. The goal of M&E is to show strong relationships among the four key variables of your impact hypothesis to help you understand how effective your L&D initiatives are. Did you accomplish your goals? Why, or why not? What can you do to improve your programs for the future? To show strong relationships, you don't always need more data; you need the right data. Only after storyboarding your preliminary M&E strategy (like Sarah and Jordan did) are you ready to select a measurement model or models and follow the tactics to fill in missing pieces of your M&E puzzle.

Finding Your Measurement Model Fit

You'll find your measurement model fit by identifying the gaps in your M&E strategy using the hypothesis framework and storyboarding strong and weak links among your four core variables. Weak links represent the missing data that you need to test your impact hypothesis. Measurement and evaluation models are designed to equip you with data, which comes in a variety of formats. Your job is to ensure you have the right data.

To select the right model, you must know what you want your data to do for you. Some models give you data to diagnose problems and source appropriate solutions. Some models help you monitor outcomes in real time. Others provide data after a program is over to summarize its effectiveness. And others give you clear insights into what worked well and what didn't and how you can improve.

Returning to Sarah and Jordan, they both thought the ROI Methodology was likely the best model for building their business case. After they used the hypothesis framework and storyboarded their M&E strategy, they discovered that the ROI Methodology was not the right model to help them fill gaps in their M&E strategy. Instead, they needed a model with clear tactics to help them show a strong relationship between how completing their improv-centered leadership development program would increase optimism, innovation, and collaboration and lead to psychological safety. That model (in my opinion) is The Measurement Map, which was developed by Bonnie Beresford. This model creates a clear chain of evidence to link learning and development initiatives and targeted performance changes.

The Measurement Map helps you translate amorphic goals (such as optimism, innovation, and collaboration) into specific activities that can actually be measured. In contrast, the ROI Methodology gives you data to establish if (and to what degree) your program provided a financial return on the total cost of the training investment.

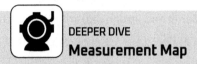

DEEPER DIVE
Measurement Map

The Measurement Map model, developed by Bonnie Beresford, can be used to create a causal chain of evidence from KSA growth to business impact. You can learn more about it at themeasurementmap.com. Also, in the appendix, you'll find an example measurement map for a sales training program from Bonnie's book *Developing Human Capital* to help you identify possible performance-focused leading indicators to monitor the effectiveness of your learning program.

Maybe one day Sarah and Jordan will invest in an in-depth ROI investigation to collect data demonstrating a compelling return that one or more organizations received by investing in their improv training program. However, what Sarah and Jordan needed right now was simply a compelling business case that used credible data to tell their program's impact story. Why is their case study a shoestring success story? They found an appropriate measurement model instead of following a common or well-established one. Applying the measurement model that fit their M&E strategy (specifically the gaps in that strategy) saved them time and required significantly fewer resources. The moral of the story for others working on a shoestring is not to use a measurement model simply because it's common or well-established. Instead, use the measurement model most aligned with your M&E goals and strategy.

TIME SAVER
Measurement Model Fit Quiz

To help you find a measurement model that fits your L&D initiatives, take the Measurement Model Fit Quiz (an online assessment I use in my impact hypothesis workshops). It uses the goals of your learning program and core challenges you face measuring and evaluating learning to identify the best model for your program. You can access the online quiz at measurementmadeeasy.com.

A Shoestring Summary

Measurement and evaluation is an ongoing process of discovery. It can be fun, and it is surely an iterative experience. Like with any project, having the right tools can make or break your M&E work. The two most important tools to begin any measurement adventure are a clear strategy and the right models to guide your thinking and generate tactics to bring your measurement strategy to life. The action steps listed here are not only a summary of takeaways from this chapter, but a guide to help you stay focused on the right measurement activities:

1. **Keep the goals of M&E top of mind.** If you're feeling ambitious, I want you to take this step right now. Find a sticky note, or simply a small piece of paper and tape. Write, "The goal of measuring and evaluating learning is to show strong relationships, not causation." Then, put it in a place where you can see it every day. M&E is a fun process of discovery. Did your learning impact hypothesis pan out like you imagined? Why or why not? What can you do to improve your learning outcomes for the future. The answers to these questions are made possible through measurement and evaluation. And, while you use thinking and concepts akin to researchers, you are not a researcher. You simply need to collect the right data to show strong relationships that indicate you are on the right track—or you aren't. Keep your M&E efforts simple. Once you get more comfortable, or perhaps find yourself in a position where you have more time and resources, you can always add more complexity later.

2. **Storyboard your M&E strategy before taking any further action.** The way L&D professionals often approach measurement and evaluation is by selecting the most common measurement model, and then following some, or all, of the steps and hoping for the best. But, this is like trying to fit a square peg into a round hole. Instead, storyboard your M&E strategy first. Use the guiding questions from the hypothesis framework to put pieces of your M&E puzzle together. It's okay to have gaps in your strategy. In fact, I expect you always will. The process of identifying those gaps will be incredibly important in finding your measurement model fit.

3. **Focus on practices and performance.** While we are all keen to show how learning initiatives can improve organizational outcomes, don't

forget that the only way learning can influence longer-term outcomes is by targeting and fostering changes in performance. Performance is simply a set of agreed upon actions and practices that people consistently engage in to drive a desired outcome. Sarah and Jordan hypothesized that incorporating improv practices would foster better leaders. What practices are critical to the outcomes your organization desires? Select measurement models and methods that help you clarify and reasonably measure the critical actions and practices needed for longer-term business outcomes to become possible.

4. **Practice asking yourself, "What data do I need to prove my hypothesis?"** Storyboarding your M&E strategy will ultimately reveal gaps in data. Good data is essential to putting your learning impact hypothesis to the test. Get comfortable asking the question, "What data do I need to prove X?" For example, "What data do I need to prove that participants who completed my improv-centered leadership development program led to increased feelings of optimism?" Or, "What data do I need to prove that participants with increased feelings of optimism were able to foster psychological safety in their workplace?" Having these questions already in mind will make it much easier to apply the tactics from your measurement model to evaluate the results of your learning program.

3
Boosting Data Literacy to Overcome Core Measurement Challenges

Data literacy. The lack of this critical skill is the root cause of our greatest obstacles to measuring learning, yet the solution is not skill development—at least not completely. ATD Research has reported numerous times (in 2009, 2016, and 2023) the correlation between limited data literacy skills and poor learning evaluation. Additionally, Josh Bersin, an iconic HR industry analyst, boldly stated in 2022 that if the HR and talent development sector doesn't expand its data literacy capabilities, it will be left behind. LinkedIn Learning's *2023 Workplace Learning Report* also revealed data literacy as a significant skill gap for L&D professionals. However, this competency gap is not unique to learning professionals, nor is it their fault that the gap exists. When you dig deeper, you find that the data literacy problem is individual and institutional. Thus, the solution to bridging this gap must be implemented systematically at the individual and institutional levels.

On the bright side, there are simple, accessible ways to incrementally bridge the data literacy gap, which I'll tackle in this chapter. But first, I'll tell you a story about data to help you start (or continue) your data literacy journey.

The Importance of Data Literacy

While chatting with a new colleague (a product developer who recently built an HR automation tool), I asked why she thought professionals struggle to show learning outcomes and impact. She responded, "HR and L&D professionals don't have the data to show stakeholders whether they are worth investing in." She's right. While I knew this from personal experience and from reading numerous research reports on the state of L&D, no one had described the problem quite like she did. Stakeholders don't know whether HR and L&D are worth investing in. What's missing that would help stakeholders know without a doubt that we are a good investment? Data proving our contribution to the business.

This conversation stirred something in me. I knew that data literacy was a problem for the industry. However, for the first time, I realized that data literacy was the one thing that differentiated high-performing, mature learning organizations from average-performing organizations.

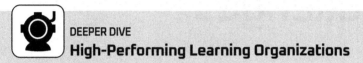

DEEPER DIVE

High-Performing Learning Organizations

The qualities and capabilities of high-performing, mature learning departments include having a secure technology infrastructure, continual funding of the L&D function (even during challenging economic times), consistent measurement systems and strategies, push and pull learning opportunities, employees taking an active role in professional development, and purposeful end-user experiences. For more information about learning maturity, check out the following research reports:

- Mind Tools for Business, *2023 Annual L&D Benchmark Report* (Edinburgh, Scotland: Mind Tools, 2023).
- Kieran King, *The Skillsoft Learning and Talent Maturity Framework: A Path to Accelerate HR's Adaptability and Your Workforce's Agility* (Nashua, NH: Skillsoft, 2020).
- Brandon Hall Group, *Learning Measurement Impact on Business Results* (Delray Beach, FL: Brandon Hall Group, 2018).
- LinkedIn Learning, *Workplace Learning Report 2024* (Sunnyvale, CA: LinkedIn Learning, 2024).

To paint a clear picture moving forward, let's pause for a moment and define data literacy. According to Gartner's information technology glossary, *data literacy* is the ability to understand different sources of data, as well as understanding the techniques used to collect and analyze data, applying these methods to a variety of use cases, and most importantly being able to read and communicate the results of data analysis in a meaningful way. One thing I would add that Gartner doesn't specifically include in its definition is the ability to use the results of data analysis to improve performance. The true value of data (and data literacy) is the insights that guide you in purposefully altering whatever you seek to change in your work. Data, when collected and analyzed correctly and with integrity, helps you see things you could not see before.

According to a recent *Forbes* article describing the value of data literacy and using data to make informed decisions, the benefits for organizations include (Nelson 2022):

- A common language among teams and departments
- Increased collaboration
- Increased curiosity, creativity, and innovation
- Cost savings

These outcomes explain why data literacy distinguishes high-performing, mature organizations from the rest. I argue these outcomes will withstand the test of time and disruption. If you tie all of them into one core value, it's alignment. A common language, increased collaboration, curiosity, creativity, and innovation are all leading indicators of organizational alignment. Organizations that are data literate and consistently use data to make informed decisions are more aligned. Department leaders are aligned. Communication is aligned, and fewer information silos exist. Employee performance is aligned with KPIs. Learning opportunities are aligned with employee and operational performance gaps. Alignment strengthens the contribution L&D makes to the business and individual employees. Organization development leaders say the value of alignment is not in achieving perfection, but in having habits and processes in place to make striving for alignment an ongoing practice (Guerra-López 2013).

Being a data-driven organization creates an environment that empowers everyone to seek, collect, and collate data to continuously improve their work. And, to no one's surprise, data-driven organizations have a more mature L&D function, are higher performing, and have lower employee turnover (Mind Tools for Business 2023a; LinkedIn Learning 2024). High-performing organizations also provide more data literacy learning opportunities compared with average-performing organizations (ATD 2023). Do you see the same light bulb I saw after my colleague dropped the "no data, no investment" statement? Increased data literacy can significantly improve many organizational outcomes, including the ability to calculate learning impact.

Now, let's discuss how to incrementally improve data literacy and solve the greatest obstacles to measuring learning impact once and for all.

Overcoming Core Obstacles to the Data Literacy Challenge

Data literacy is the key to breaking free from the struggle to show the value of learning as an organization development tool. However, we can't simply snap our fingers and become data literate. (Wouldn't that be nice!) There are a few important building blocks that must be in place before we can adopt data best practices and use data to make agile and informed decisions.

Every several years, ATD Research surveys learning professionals to explore their approach and the greatest barriers to measuring learning impact. The same three challenges are consistently reported over 14 years of research, with the number 1 challenge being isolating training impact from other factors (Table 3-1).

Table 3-1. Persistent Challenges to M&E According to ATD Research

2009	2016	2023
• Isolating training impact from other factors • Technology used to deliver training doesn't feature useful evaluation tools • Evaluation data is not standardized enough to compare well across functions	• Isolating training impact from other factors • Don't have access to the necessary data • Technology used to deliver training doesn't feature useful evaluation tools	• Isolating training impact from other factors • Lack of infrastructure or knowledge to integrate learning data with other org data • Don't have access to the necessary data

To explore challenges in measuring and evaluating learning, ATD Research asks participants a closed-ended question that requires them to select an option from a predetermined list. Other studies have been done over the years using a qualitative approach to uncovering measurement and evaluation challenges. These studies reveal similar yet distinctly different obstacles.

To dig deeper and go beyond the quantitative research, I did a qualitative study on measurement challenges experienced by L&D professionals across the globe. I interviewed 40 learning leaders and practitioners to understand common challenges to measuring and evaluating learning. The stories they shared confirmed my own frustrations were experienced by many others in organizations of all shapes and sizes. Interestingly, these challenges revealed root causes of long-term quantitative trends in measuring learning impact. Solving these core challenges forms the fundamental infrastructure for becoming data literate and a data-driven organization or individual. Root causes of long-term measurement challenges include:

- Over-emphasis on knowledge-based learning design
- Lack of strategy
- Lack of buy-in and support from stakeholders

Let's tackle each one in turn, and then cover some solutions to boost your comfort working with data and your approach to measurement.

Expanding Beyond Knowledge-Based Approaches to L&D

One of the first clients in my consulting practice hired me to translate his expertise working as a one-on-one coach into a cohort-course. The goal of his coaching experience was for participants to improve their profit margin by learning how to better manage their revenue and expenses. When I asked him what prevented his target audience from appropriately managing their revenue and expenses, he said they didn't know the right tools or technology to manage their finances. So, the hypothesis going into the project was that if participants were given the tools, technology, and a supportive environment to practice using those tools, they would improve their profit margin.

He put this hypothesis to the test by designing a pilot program, which received great satisfaction scores. Feeling encouraged, he translated the live cohort into a series of on-demand videos plus monthly group coaching. Over time, he learned that the biggest barrier to appropriately managing revenue and expenses was not a lack of knowledge, tools, or technology; it was lack of a good bookkeeper. This client has since shifted the focus of his business to providing fractional, affordable bookkeeping services for entrepreneurs with à la carte educational videos to supplement knowledge gaps as needed. What he originally believed was a knowledge gap turned out to be something else entirely!

One of my favorite books, written by L&D professional Julie Dirksen, is *Design for How People Learn*. Dirksen reminds readers there are only a few levers to pull when filling the gap between where people are now (in competencies and performance) and where they want or need to be. Those levers are knowledge, skills, motivation, habits, environment, and communication. In the L&D industry, we overemphasize knowledge-focused solutions by regularly assuming that competency and performance gaps will be solved by acquiring new knowledge. However, knowledge (information and curated content) is only a small fraction of what people truly need to bridge performance gaps.

The experience I gained working with my first client continues to be an unforgettable reminder that I have to validate my hunches. For many L&D professionals, it might be frightening to ask stakeholders or SMEs for data confirming that the solution they believe is right will truly accomplish their long-term goals. Yet, too often, you can waste time and money investing in knowledge-based solutions only to find out later that a different lever was needed to influence the desired outcomes. If we aren't designing learning to change behavior or improve performance, then there will be no business impact to measure.

Impact is the longer-term consequence made possible only when the performance or behavioral outcomes are consistently maintained. David James (2016), chief learning officer at 360Learning and contributor to the Learning Guild, pointedly summarizes this predicament: "Courses and classrooms seem to have confused the job of L&D with education. At school and at college, the aim is to instill knowledge. At work, the aim of L&D is to improve performance and build capability to deliver on operational and strategic goals." If we're designing to improve knowledge, the only outcomes we'll achieve are changes in knowledge. For long-term impact, we must design learning content that changes behavior and performance.

Dirksen (2015) recommends we first identify the cause of performance gaps before we design, develop, and deliver any learning initiative. It's important to note that there are likely multiple contributors to performance gaps. In my 20 years of experience as a teacher, curriculum writer, instructional designer, and training director, I've observed the three most likely culprits to be environment, motivation, and habits. To validate the root cause of performance gaps, we must leverage data literacy and a good old fashioned needs assessment. This doesn't have to take an immense amount of time. However, you will surely waste time by creating an impartial solution to performance problems if you don't get the right information and insight to influence the performance outcomes you desire.

If you return to Table 3-1, you'll notice that isolating the effects of training from other variables is the number 1 challenge observed over more than 14 years of research. It's my assertion (stemming from the many research articles I've read and my own experience as a learning professional) that we intuitively recognize that knowledge alone is not sufficient to influence performance and business outcomes. Yet, you may be stuck in an environment (or with a boss or a status quo) that pushes you into the role of information distributor, content creator, and knowledge bearer. You know that role and that type of learning initiative will not have the long-term impact you desire. If you could somehow isolate the effects of training, you might be able to prove that the status quo—overemphasizing knowledge-based learning—isn't working! I imagine the other reason you want to isolate training's effect from other variables is to calculate the unique contribution of training and learning to the business. I invite you to think about isolating the effects of training from a different perspective.

We can increase the likelihood of a learning initiative's success (or learning contributing to some meaningful change in performance and in business) if a few key variables are present, such as participant motivation, manager support, stakeholder buy-in, having the right knowledge, participants' efficacy in performance, and access to the proper tools (Tannenbaum et al. 1993). Thus, research corroborates that knowledge alone isn't sufficient to influence behavior change and learning transfer.

Isolating the effects of training and learning sets you up for success when calculating the ROI of training. While the ability to calculate ROI is historically the gold standard of learning evaluation, there is another standard I would like to see used more often: strategically combining the powers of learning with other organization development initiatives. This is in fact the opposite of isolating the effects of training from other variables. We know that knowledge alone isn't sufficient to influence behavior change. We know that the alignment of many factors outside L&D's direct control increases the success of our learning initiatives. Why not lead with a collaborative approach to designing learning solutions versus trying to isolate the effects of learning? For professionals working on a shoestring (or any learning professional), a collaborative approach maximizes access to resources and significantly increases results.

Two measurement advisors, Kevin M. Yates (also known as the L&D detective) and Kristopher Newbauer (author of the book *Aligning Instructional Design With Business Goals*), also encourage this collaborative approach to learning design and evaluation. Kevin describes a collaborative approach to learning design as a cross-functional contribution to achieving business goals. Kristopher encourages readers to work with stakeholders to estimate the contribution different departments or initiatives (including L&D) have toward key drivers of business outcomes. This cross-functional approach to learning design recognizes that training alone cannot (and should not) influence business outcomes. Your influence is more powerful when strategically combined. Instead of striving to measure a training program's unique impact on the business, you can work alongside other organizational leaders to come up with appropriate metrics to demonstrate how each department or initiative contributed to desired business goals.

 DEEPER DIVE
Implementing Cross-Functional Learning Design and Measurement

You can learn more about Kevin M. Yates's approach to cross-functional measurement on his website at kevinmyates.com and Kristopher Newbauer's approach by reading chapter 6, "Define Success," in his 2023 book, *Aligning Instructional Design With Business Goals*.

Overcoming a Lack of Strategy

In the same way that overuse of knowledge-based learning can hold you back, so does a lack of strategy. In my qualitative study, 35 percent of participants reported that a lack of strategy was a barrier to demonstrating learning outcomes (Szlachta 2022). One participant working in the pharmaceutical industry said, "L&D is an organizational resource that has not been historically measured in terms of the returns . . . on the investment." Another participant from the public health industry shared, "We need to change the culture of L&D to be less people pleasing and more strategic." While the professionals in my study were specifically referring to strategy limitations at the department or industry level, the lack of structured organizational focus and competing priorities are also cited as significant barriers to implementing learning measurement in other quantitative studies (Mercer Mettl 2022; Lea and Ells 2022). Thus, to overcome M&E barriers once and for all, we must improve strategic thinking and planning.

In chapters 1 and 2, I shared numerous ways you can improve strategic thinking and planning via the impact hypothesis and by distinguishing measurement strategy from tactics. If you incorporate the best practices from those chapters, your data literacy muscles will surely grow! In a book focused on measurement strategies for professionals working on a shoestring, it is my goal to help you focus your time, energy, and resources on getting the greatest value out of your investment in measurement. Therefore, there are a few other measurement strategy best practices I'm eager to share in the next few sections. Incorporating them into your M&E work will also boost your data literacy skills.

Prioritize Your Evaluation Resources

I often start my conference presentations with this question: "Should we measure and evaluate everything?" It always sparks lively debate among participants. There is a well-documented gap between what CEOs want and what L&D delivers through data demonstrating the business impact of learning. Ninety-six percent of CEOs want data on the business impact of learning, and only 9 to 38 percent of learning professionals consistently measure business impact (Phillips 2010; Brandon Hall Group 2020; ATD 2016). With these statistics, it's easy to feel immense pressure to evaluate the business impact of everything. In truth, this is a waste of time and resources. Every learning initiative does not matter equally. We should prioritize our measurement energy. Invest your time and resources wisely by answering this question: Is the goal or purpose of this learning initiative to disseminate information or facilitate change?

If you're immediately thinking, "Wait. Isn't it possible for one learning initiative to have both goals?" It's not! Disseminating information is always part of the process of facilitating change; however, facilitating change is not required to disseminate information. Thus, your initiative is either designed to share information, such as compliance training, or to create change, such as performance improvement. You don't need to invest strategic energy evaluating training that disseminates information, but you will need a solid strategy to evaluate the effectiveness and outcomes of initiatives designed to facilitate change.

Take compliance training, which makes up nearly 70 percent of training programs in most organizations (Talent LMS and SHRM 2022). You don't typically need to show the outcomes, results, or impact of training that is done solely for compliance purposes. You can evaluate the training program for learner satisfaction, completion rate, and engagement or participation barriers. In most cases, the only data you need to capture for compliance programs is proof that a targeted group of employees was given access to and reviewed the necessary information. This can be done formally using a DocuSign (or equivalent e-signature platform) approach. Informally, you can use metadata with programs like Microsoft SharePoint and Google Workspace to see which employees accessed specific documents and, in some cases, for what length of time. However, you do not need to invest energy, time, or scarce resources tracking impact for compliance programs. While your percentage may vary, this means only approximately 30 percent of your programs actually need measurement strategies to show performance changes and business impact. Does this information make you feel relieved? I hope so!

Invest in Strategy First—Technology Second

In the L&D sector, we often have a bad reputation of succumbing to shiny object syndrome when working with technology. We've had a "tech is the magic solution" glimmer in our eyes since the 1920s and '30s when radio was predicted to revolutionize education. Radio, television, and now social media have surely revolutionized how information is distributed, but experienced L&D professionals know that information distribution does not guarantee learning.

DEEPER DIVE
Avoid the Shiny New Learning Technology Object

Read the first chapter of (or the entire book) *E-Learning and the Science of Instruction* by Ruth C. Clark and Richard E. Mayer for a fascinating overview of historical beliefs about how technology would revolutionize education. You'll find that while technology tools constantly evolve, the science behind good learning remains the same. While many L&D professionals adopt technology and forsake the science behind good learning, this trend seems to be counterbalancing in recent years.

To preserve learning's value to the business, avoid being swayed by shiny objects. Investing in the right technology at the right time is an important step toward your team becoming a mature learning function. However, if you aren't ready to optimally adopt tech, you will waste time and money. This moves you in the opposite direction of showing stakeholders that L&D is a worthy investment.

While learning management systems (LMS), learning experience platforms (LXP), and learning record stores (LRS) can be useful, they are not currently equipped to automatically provide data on learning outcomes or impact. I've seen countless tech platforms advertise their ability to demonstrate the ROI of L&D through their analytics. They feature output metrics like engagement, completion, and net promoter scores (NPS), and then call this data learning impact. However, that data on its own won't tell you anything about performance and business impact. To collect outcome and impact data, you must build intentional data collection systems inside or alongside digital tools like an LMS, LXP, or LRS platform to capture changes in performance activities.

So, rather than starting with a tech-first approach to capturing data, look to the hypothesis framework (featured in chapter 1) for the data you need, and then identify which technology tools can help you capture that data. You might learn that what you already have in your tech ecosystem will suit your needs. If not, you might need to complement what you have with a new tool. (Chapter 8 will provide guidance on making tech decisions.)

Ask the Right Questions

When my good friend and colleague Dan Bennett of Video for Entrepreneurs sent a feedback survey to the latest graduates of his cohort course and got a nearly 100 percent response rate, he needed my help. He wondered what to do with all that information.

Dan's spreadsheet contained 10 responses to 12 open-ended questions. That equates to 120 cells of rich qualitative data. Anyone looking at this spreadsheet would be overwhelmed.

Dan, like many others working on a shoestring, is a department of one. He is the sole owner-operator of a small business offering courses, consulting, and coaching to help entrepreneurs look and sound good on camera. He cares deeply about creating great results for his customers, and he is always seeking feedback to improve his program. However, he also has a tight timeline, no budget for M&E, and very little experience measuring learning programs. In addition, he was working in a market in which the needs of his customers (that is, his learners) were constantly changing.

The first version of Dan's course evaluation strategy was a 12-question survey asking for self-reported anecdotes describing how participants thought they changed after the course was over. He also included feedback questions that were intuitive to the reader and were clearly written with the intention of improving the program. Sounds like a viable shoestring solution, right? Absolutely—if he asked the right questions. Unfortunately, he didn't.

There are an infinite number of ways to pose a question. In the M&E world—especially when you're working on a shoestring—there is a right way that can save you an immense amount of time in the data analysis phase. Asking the wrong questions can leave you overwhelmed and less likely to glean any meaningful insights from your surveys (or other data collection methods).

To save time in the most important phase of evaluation (data analysis), incorporate a few key best practices when posing questions. Your questions should be:

- Written to provide data showing if the program accomplished its goals
- Predominantly closed-ended (except for cases when you are intentionally looking for narrative responses)
- Worded clearly and objectively (not leading the responder to answer a certain way)

- Asked at the right time for you to track growth or change
- Formatted to easily observe insights you need from the data
- Generate actionable feedback to improve future programs

Let's reflect on the criteria for asking the right questions and review Dan's questions. In Table 3-2, you'll find Dan's original questions, examples of how to revise them to improve his survey to get better data, and some detailed explanations.

Table 3-2. Implementing Best Practices for Survey Questions

Summative Questions *(These questions invite participants to reflect on the overall learning experience.)*		
Original Questions	**Revised Questions**	**Explanation**

• Overall, how would you rate the quality of the course content on a scale of 1-10? Why?
• Did the course meet your expectations? Please explain why.
• Would you recommend this course to a colleague or friend? Why or why not?
	• Please rate the overall quality of the Video for Entrepreneurs Program. If you selected the third option, please share why the program did not meet your expectations and what could be improved.
	  ◦ High quality. The program met or exceeded my expectations.
	  ◦ Average quality. The program was good, but not great.
	  ◦ Low quality. The program did not meet my expectations.
	• How likely are you to recommend this program to a colleague or friend? (Answer options include a 10-point Likert scale to calculate an NPS*.)
		Dan originally included summative questions at the start and end of the survey. However, they should be placed at the beginning of the survey. Instead of asking his three original questions, Dan should ask one or both of the revised versions.
		
		*There is much debate about using NPS to evaluate learning programs. I don't think NPS offers valuable information if you're evaluating higher education or corporate learning. If you are selling a program to customers as a learning product, then NPS scores are more relevant because they are a marketing metric that customers expect to see when deciding whether to purchase your program.

Table 3-2. (cont.)

Goal Evaluation Questions *(These questions help evaluate whether the program accomplished its goals.)*		
Original Questions	**Revised Questions**	**Explanation**
• If you could describe your businesses being successful after implementing video, what does that look like? • Do you have a better understanding of what it takes to succeed through creating video content? • Have you successfully created and published any videos since completing the course? If so, how many? • Did the course meet your professional development needs?	• How often do you feel stuck, hopeless, or overwhelmed when you think about creating videos? (Answer option was a 5-point frequency scale.) • How often do you feel alone or helpless when you create video content? (Answer option was a 5-point frequency scale.) • I have a clear plan or strategy for creating my video content. (Answer option was a 5-point agree-or-disagree scale.) • I am confident on camera. (Answer option was a 5-point agree-or-disagree scale.) • I am proud of the videos I produce. (Answer option was a 5-point agree-or-disagree scale.) • I have a good system or rhythm to stay motivated and consistent with my video content. (Answer option was a 5-point agree-or-disagree scale.)	Dan initially sprinkled goal evaluation questions throughout the survey. Instead, he should begin the survey with questions inviting participants to reflect on their growth and accomplishments. Ask these at the start of the program and at anticipated key growth milestones. Dan included two video portfolio projects as part of the program, so he was able to ask the post-questions after participants completed each portfolio project. In addition to these revised questions, Dan also created a separate assessment to evaluate the quality of the videos that participants created during the program. The assessment was completed by the instructor, video creator, and all other course participants to show growth, from multiple perspectives in video quality over time.

Table 3-2. (cont.)

Participant Progress Analysis *(These questions help calculate the relationship between course completion and goal achievement.)*		
Original Questions	**Revised Questions**	**Explanation**
• Did you make progress as a result of taking action and doing the coursework?	Instead of relying on self-reported responses, to analyze the relationship between course completion and goal achievement, Dan and I created an average course completion score and an average goal achievement score for every participant. Then, we explored if there was a positive relationship between course completion and goal achievement.	Dan's original progress analysis question relied on the participant's self-reported response. Ideally, you shouldn't use self-reported responses to calculate the relationship between course completion and growth or change. By using average course completion and average goal achievement scores, Dan could determine that there was a strong probability (that is, a correlation) that program participation influenced growth and change.
Learning Experience Feedback Questions *(These questions help gather feedback to improve the content and delivery of the program.)*		
Original Questions	**Revised Questions**	**Explanation**
• Were you able to complete the course assignments before the beginning of the next class? • Was the course instructor available and approachable for questions and support? • Was the course missing something you considered important? If so, what should have been included? • Do you have any additional thoughts about the course?	We did not change any of Dan's original questions in this section because the data he received from his questions provided useful and actionable feedback to improve the program for future participants.	These questions are ideally positioned in the final section of your survey, after goal evaluation and participant progress questions. Dan asked feedback questions based on the challenges he had experienced in previous programs. Your feedback questions should be written to offer insight and ideas for improving future programs. They will be based on your own program structure, content, and delivery methods.

After Dan reached out to me for help, we worked together to create an improved evaluation plan for his next cohort. The process of refining his evaluation plan also led to refining the program content and delivery. By the end of his next cohort, he could clearly see that participants who completed 80 to 100 percent of his program met or highly surpassed the growth goals he envisioned for his customers. And, because he took an hour to reformat his assessment plan, he saved numerous hours doing data analysis to uncover these program outcomes.

The most important changes we made to Dan's feedback survey (which will help you write better questions and get more useful data) were adding context to the survey, using open-ended questions sparingly and intentionally, asking questions at the right time to track growth and change, and formatting survey questions to make data analysis easier.

Add Context to Your Survey

Include a brief narrative that ties all the questions together. Remember our discussion about the impact hypothesis, outlining what we're doing and why, from the first two chapters? Include some of the details from your impact hypothesis in your survey so participants clearly understand the outcomes and purpose of the program.

This context combined with the right survey structure—summative questions, followed by goal evaluation questions, participant progress questions, and then learning experience feedback questions—also helps reinforce the intended goals of the program and provide an opportunity for participants to reflect on their accomplishments.

Use Open-Ended Questions Sparingly and Intentionally

In Dan's original survey, only one of his 12 questions was closed-ended. You can understand why he was overwhelmed by all the qualitative data he received. There was a lot of text in one spreadsheet. The greatest downside of open-ended questions is that it takes more time for participants to write their responses. In turn, this can lead to lower quality data and lower survey response rates. In addition, you must do extra work to find themes in the responses to make the qualitative data useful. Save your open-ended questions for testimonials, personal impact stories, and feedback for improving the program.

Ask Questions at the Right Time to Track Growth and Change

Dan only administered his original survey after the program was over. Thus, he was unable to compare participants' knowledge, attitudes, or skills before and after the program. Ideally, we use assessments and surveys multiple times throughout a program to show growth and change over time.

Contrary to what you might think, the most important times to collect data are not before and immediately after a program; instead, the best time will depend on when you anticipate participants experiencing growth because of the learning experience. Therefore, you need to identify growth milestones before you deliver a program and then insert strategic assessments and surveys to capture growth during anticipated growth milestones.

Format Survey Questions to Make Data Analysis Easier

To create the best question format and answer options, we first need to know what participants' cumulative answers should tell us. For example, we reformatted this question from Dan's original survey for easier analysis: "Did you make progress because you completed your coursework?" In truth, we didn't need to ask this question to find out if people who completed their coursework made progress. Thus, in the revised survey, we eliminated it. What Dan wanted to know was if there was a strong relationship between people achieving the goals of his course (making progress) and completing the coursework. We didn't need to ask participants this question to explore the relationship between the course completion rate and the course outcomes. Instead, we could use course activity metadata to generate a completion score and compare that rate to participants' goals and accomplishments.

Here's another good example of how reformatting two more of Dan's original questions made analysis easier: "Did the course meet your expectations? Please explain why," and "Overall, how would you rate the quality of the course content on a scale of 1–10? Why?" Both questions are open-ended and make data analysis more difficult than it needs to be. By merging them into one closed-ended question with an optional open-ended follow-up question, we made data collection easier for the participant and analysis easier for ourselves.

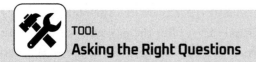

TOOL
Asking the Right Questions

In the appendix, you'll find a question criteria checklist you can consult whenever you're building evaluation survey questions (or any questions for that matter).

Use Self-Reported Data With Caution

Will Thalheimer (2018), creator of the Learning Transfer Evaluation Model (LTEM), says, "When we ask learners whether a learning intervention will improve their job performance, we are getting their Level 1 reactions. We are NOT getting Level 3 (behavior and performance change) data. More specifically, we are not getting information we can trust to tell us whether a person's on-the-job behavior has improved due to the learning intervention." Thalheimer directs us to a core challenge of using self-reported data to measure and evaluate behavior and performance change. Can you use self-reporting to collect trustworthy data showing behavior and performance changes after learning?

Let me introduce you to Larry Mohl, who founded the change experience platform Rali. He needed to use self-reporting to capture behavior change after a three-month inclusion-focused leadership development program, but he wasn't sure how to ensure the data was credible. He initially wanted to use observation as his evaluation technique, but this proved infeasible due to limited staff resources and expertise (a typical shoestring dilemma). Another alternative, peer or supervisor feedback, was similarly shot down due to time limitations. He also didn't have any key performance metrics assigned to the leadership development program to review before and after evaluations. Thus, a self-assessment was the best option for the situation.

To use self-reporting and collect data that is trustworthy, you must wear a researcher's hat. There are two research best practices that you can easily incorporate into a self-reported evaluation plan to significantly increase the quality and credibility of your data: identifying microbehaviors and data triangulation.

TIME SAVER
Common Evaluation Methods

Self-reported surveys are just one method for evaluating programs (whether it is a learning program, marketing initiative, or government-based development opportunity). Here are a handful of the most common evaluation methods (some of which you'll be familiar with, and others you may not think of as evaluation methods). Chapter 8 goes into detail about how to use the right tech platforms for each of these evaluation methods.

- Observations
- Psychometric assessments
- Exams or quizzes
- Role plays
- Simulations
- Projects or portfolios
- Presentations
- Case studies
- Feedback from mentors, supervisors, or peers
- Self-assessments
- Goal versus actual in key performance metrics

Identifying Microbehaviors

Identifying microbehaviors is especially important when measuring the outcomes of soft-skills training. These would be programs that develop capabilities such as leadership, communication, diversity and inclusion, mentoring, and conflict resolution.

You know the familiar adage: Begin with the end in mind. Employing microbehaviors in evaluation requires you to clarify (before the design, delivery, and evaluation of the program) what behaviors you want participants to employ in the workplace (or their everyday lives). This is when my work with Larry began. Luckily for me, his instructional design team had already identified behavioral outcomes for their inclusion program. They targeted eight inclusive behavior categories that were then broken into one to three microbehaviors. For example, the empathetic listening behavior category included three microbehavior descriptions, including "When I listen to someone's story or circumstances, I try to understand how they felt and what they experienced in that situation." These microbehaviors were taught, practiced, and reinforced throughout the training program.

DEEPER DIVE
The DACUM Model

If you struggle identifying the microbehaviors central to your learning program's (and business's) success, use the DACUM model, which stands for develop a curriculum. This model is a collaborative approach that involves working with high performers to unpack the "secret sauce" of actions and behaviors leading to business KPIs, including customer satisfaction and retention, sales, productivity, and employee engagement. To learn more, read the 2020 book *DACUM: The Designers Guide to Curriculum Development* by Robert E. Adams, R. Lance Hogan, and Luke J. Steinke.

By clarifying the microlevel behavior change you wish to achieve after the completion of a development program, you'll not only tailor the learning experience, but you'll also be able to easily incorporate those microbehaviors into your evaluation plan. Once you've identified which behaviors to include in your self-assessment survey, you're ready to incorporate the next best practice: data triangulation. And that's just what Larry and I did.

Data Triangulation

Data triangulation is the process of intentionally collecting different data sources or formats to evaluate the same outcome. It's akin to asking four different people who witnessed a car accident (from four different street corners) to share their experience of what happened. The elements that show up consistently as each person shares their perspective will have more significance, because they were shared by four independent sources. For data triangulation to be effective, you want to use different sources and types of data. If different data sources and formats reveal a similar outcome, your evaluation's result has more credibility. You can increase the trustworthiness of your data through triangulation.

Larry's evaluation was a true shoestring case. He had limited time to develop the evaluation and administer it to hundreds of employees. Thus, collecting data in different formats was not an option. However, he could leverage different sources of qualitative and quantitative data. And, the best part, he could collect all sources of data with one survey.

So, what did Larry's final self-reported evaluation survey look like? The survey compared how frequently program participants practiced the microbehaviors before they began the leadership program and after they completed the program. Because they did not do any baseline assessments prior to completing the program, the next best option was to invite participants to reflect on their experience before they received training to estimate how often they practiced inclusion. I don't recommend that you use this approach regularly or have participants estimate the frequency of specific behaviors or practices. It's always best to capture baseline data before a program begins.

Larry's survey strategically formatted preprogram frequency questions into a matrix (Table 3-3). Postprogram questions, on the other hand, were grouped according to behavioral category and presented one at a time, which enabled Larry to collect qualitative data along with quantitative data.

Table 3-3. Behavior Change Evaluation Plan Using Self-Reported Data

Before beginning the leadership program, how often were you using the following actions and behaviors when engaging in one-on-one conversations with colleagues or during team meetings?					
Action or Behavior	**Never**	**Sometimes**	**Often**	**Regularly**	**Always**
When I listen to someone's story or circumstances, I try to understand how they felt and what experienced in that situation.					

We randomly selected a handful of postprogram frequency questions and then asked open-ended follow-up questions.

- When participants indicated the frequency of the behavior was never or sometimes, we asked, "What got in the way or made it difficult for you to practice this behavior in one-on-one conversations with colleagues or in team meetings?"
- When participants indicated the frequency was regularly or always, we asked, "What helped you or made it easy for you to practice this behavior in one-on-one conversations with colleagues or in team meetings?" and "What changes have you observed with your

organization, team, or your interpersonal relationships because you've been applying this microbehavior?"

If participants indicated the frequency was regularly or always, we also asked a closed-ended question using a list of predetermined short-term or long-term outcomes. For example, we asked, "Please select all that apply. What changes have you observed with your organization, team, or your interpersonal relationships because you've been applying this microbehavior?" The drop-down menu included things like improved relationships among team members, improved morale on the team, increased team productivity, and reduction in conflict among team members.

Larry wanted to use self-reporting to explore not only what specific microbehaviors were being practiced after the leadership program, but also how frequently people were practicing those behaviors. In addition, he wanted to test the hypothesis his stakeholders had about long-term outcomes that might occur for the organization once people had been practicing inclusive behaviors. Inviting participants to reflect on microbehaviors and formatting the survey to capture both qualitative and quantitative data increased his confidence in the self-reported data's trustworthiness.

In addition, we asked some participants to respond to questions with qualitative answers, and others to respond to the same question using a multi-selection answer choice. We could then compare how qualitative responses lined up with the quantitative multiselection responses. If qualitative responses using the participant's own words correlated strongly with the selections other respondents made in the multiselection question, we had high confidence that the outcome was valid. In addition, this survey was administered to a group of more than 300 employees. The credibility of self-reported data increases with a larger sample size.

TOOL
Self-Reported Behavior Change Evaluation Plan

In the appendix, you'll find a template to create your own self-reported behavior change evaluation plan.

So, it's possible to use self-assessments to collect trustworthy data. You simply need to think like a researcher and follow best practices to minimize bias in the most biased form of data collection—self-reporting.

Overcoming a Lack of Buy-In and Support From Stakeholders

Early studies on training transfer, effectiveness, and learning measurement dating back to the 1980s began reporting a trend that is still pervasive in the L&D industry today (Baldwin et al. 2009). Company leaders aren't concerned about training transfer. Stakeholders accept L&D as a cost of doing business but not as a strategic partner in operational success. Approximately 50 percent of business leaders don't think measuring learning outcomes is important (IFP 2022). Does this sound familiar to you? It is my hope that anyone reading this book five to 10 years from now will answer this question with a resounding no. Sadly, we aren't there yet. Over the past few decades, L&D professionals have consistently reported limited support from business leaders.

This is not true for all organizations. However, it is true for many companies around the globe. Of the 40 participants I interviewed in my qualitative study, 80 percent reported a less-than-ideal organizational environment and relationship with stakeholders that contributed to limitations measuring learning outcomes (Szlachta 2022). In addition, organizations with less mature learning departments experienced a lack of partnership at a higher rate than businesses with mature learning departments. Thus, building relationships with stakeholders is incredibly important for learning professionals working on a shoestring. As my colleague shared at the start of this chapter, stakeholders commonly don't know whether L&D is a worthy investment for the business. To build stronger relationships, we need to think more like business professionals and start amassing the right data to show our value to business leaders. Remember, data literacy is the key.

Stakeholders and learning professionals are equally responsible for the sad state of our partnership. Both parties can make significant strides to create trusting, cooperative relationships. Because this trend is decades in the making and arguably the most significant barrier to measuring and evaluating learning, I've devoted an entire chapter to developing buy-in and partnerships with stakeholders. If this topic interests you, you'll greatly enjoy chapter 6.

A Shoestring Summary

In the introduction, I mentioned that it is possible to measure and evaluate learning programs on a shoestring, and doing so requires only one thing: thinking differently about M&E. There are many concepts in this chapter that are contrary to the status quo, and I sincerely hope they have inspired you to open your mind to new ways of approaching measurement. The following action list includes the most critical steps to take after reading this chapter; doing so will not only challenge you to think differently, but will expand your data literacy too:

1. **Collaboration gets you on the fast track to data literacy.** If *Forbes* reports that data-driven organizations are more collaborative, communicative, and aligned, then I think it's possible the reverse can also be true. Organizations that may need to up their data-literacy game can strategically lean into collaboration, communication, and alignment to boost their data-driven practices. Instead of operating in isolation, lean into cross-functional and cross-departmental collaboration. Design learning and measurement strategies that complement other department initiatives. When asked to create training, turn to your department leaders to learn how the training request aligns with their initiatives and priorities to optimize and maximize your impact.

2. **Practice refining your survey questions to simplify data analysis.** One of my favorite exercises is to take a survey or questionnaire, go through each question, randomly select a response from the list of options, and ask myself, "If 50 percent of people responded X, what does that tell me? How can I use this information to improve my program?" If I don't know what to do with the data, then it's time to refine my question.

3. **Find ways to incorporate data triangulation.** Most of your data collection is likely yielding self-reported data. After all, self-reported data is the easiest to collect. Opting for this approach is a cost-effective option for professionals working on a shoestring. However, without triangulation, your data might be overly biased and thus not tell you anything valid or reliable.

PART II
BORROW

It's easy to overcomplicate measurement and evaluation. In part 1 of this book, we covered fundamental concepts and methodologies. Now, we'll dive into opportunities to borrow the wisdom of others, leverage data you already have to show program outcomes and impact, and save time by integrating and eliminating steps in both the measurement and instructional design processes. We don't need to reinvent the wheel. All we need to do is challenge the status quo and stop doing things just because that's the way they've always been done.

In this part of the book, you'll explore how to:

- Save time by integrating measurement, evaluation, and instructional design.
- Use data you already have to evaluate and improve your programs.

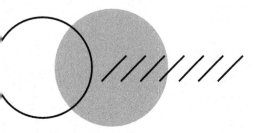

4
Saving Time by Integrating Measurement With Instructional Design

Have you ever attended a Cirque du Soleil performance? I saw them one time when they came to Austin, Texas. Throughout the entire show, my jaw dropped while I wondered, "How are they doing that?" The performers were so in sync with one another, the music, and the lights. It was truly a grand production. If a performer, light or sound technician, or prop on stage was out of place, the result could be disastrous. All the thoughtful details came together at the right place and right time to make this magnificent showcase of talent possible.

For a learning program to be successful and create its intended impact, it must be aligned with the precision of a Cirque du Soleil performance. In place of performers, technicians, and props, learning professionals must align learner characteristics (abilities, personalities, experience, self-efficacy, and demographics), organizational dynamics, instructional design best practices, technology, scheduling, stakeholder expectations, and so much more. It's a wonder that any learning program is successful at all. And it's no mystery why you might be hesitant to measure program outcomes. The chance of being perfectly successful is unlikely. However, measurement and evaluation are the tools that will help you incrementally improve your programs and continuously strive for Cirque du Soleil–like alignment.

So, what exactly should we be striving to incrementally improve? Value. More specifically, improving (by reducing) the amount of time it takes for learning to create value for individuals, organizations, or communities. Value shows up in many ways, and the value associated with learning can be highly subjective (especially for individuals). Some people will argue that we shouldn't try to quantify the value of learning because it is unique to each person. That is true. I think the long-term impact of learning is unique for everyone. However, the immediate and medium-term outcomes of education and learning, which show up before long-term impact, are often consistent, similar, and sometimes even predictable.

While the value of learning can take many forms, I argue there are two primary ways it takes shape: face value and deeper value. The *face value of learning* is the successful distribution of new information. This is face value because we don't have any specific expectations for what people will do with the new information. Simply having access to the information is intrinsically valuable. Measuring the face value of learning involves collecting evidence to prove that the targeted group received the intended information. On the other hand, the *deeper value of learning* is what becomes possible when new information is correctly understood and then accurately applied in real life. Outcomes can be tangible (such as physical products, currency, or specific deliverables) or intangible (such as decisions, relationships, or strategies; Binder 2017). Measuring the deeper value of learning involves knowing in advance what you want to become possible through a learning experience and collecting evidence to prove those tangible and intangible possibilities occurred.

Historically, the time it takes to prove the deeper value of learning to individuals, organizations, and communities—what is known as "time to value" (TTV)—is quite extensive. There are many variables and processes involved in creating learning content that offers deeper value. We can save time and easily prioritize resources by inspecting the alignment of these variables and the processes commonly used to develop learning. Integrating instructional design, measurement, and evaluation is a key strategy in reducing TTV—without sacrificing any of the value.

Time-Saving Benefits of Clarity

In a new client discovery call, I was listening for evidence that my client, Kathy, wanted to develop a learning program for either face value (sharing good information) or deeper value (changing behavior). She told me about her desire to create a program based on the principles written in her book to help others make big personal decisions with their heart, mind, and body aligned. Clearly, she was committed to offering a deeper value of learning, and the core behavior she sought to change was improving decision-making practices.

She had a detailed curriculum outline, and the featured information was novel and interesting. Yet, after I reviewed it, I couldn't see how all the information included in the curriculum would help people make decisions with their mind, heart, and body aligned. She hadn't organized her program around building the practice of making aligned decisions. She'd only selected the tools and frameworks that were most influential from her life experience and focused on teaching one tool per week for four weeks. Thus, while she'd done a great job organizing a learning program that would share great information, it wasn't designed to help people change their decision-making behaviors.

How could Kathy redesign her program to increase the chances of predictably improving participants' satisfaction with their big life decisions? She needed to align her learning content, activities, and evaluation strategies to be laser focused on supporting people in improving their decision-making practices. To align her content, activities, and measurement strategy, we completed the following exercise:

1. **Find the problem.** What is the problem with how people currently make big decisions in their life? According to Kathy, people commonly looked outside themselves for answers and ended up making decisions they were unhappy with.

2. **Confirm the greatest pain point perpetuating the problem.** What contributed to people lacking confidence and feeling unhappy with their decisions? Kathy thought that people relied too heavily on friends, family, and external circumstances in their decision-making process. If they could increase confidence using internal influences when making big life decisions, they would be happier.

3. **Clarify what people should be doing differently.** What could people do differently to improve their confidence and satisfaction with their big life decisions? From Kathy's experience, people should understand their core values and make decisions through the lens

of those values. They should also incorporate energy management, positive intelligence, and emotional intelligence into their decision-making activities.

4. **Find a method of evaluating whether people are practicing the ideal behaviors.** How will you know if people are already incorporating these actions into their decision-making practice? How can you evaluate whether people are changing their practices and if they truly feel happier? Kathy thought that people let too many outside influences inform their decisions, versus reflecting internally. If she could track the ratio of internal influences and external influences as people make decisions, she could potentially see whether, over time, people were using more internal influences versus external influences. That would be a good indicator that people were moving in the right direction with their decision-making practices.

5. **Prioritize the content, practice activities, and performance support needed to bring about the desired change.** What information and practice opportunities are essential for people to build a more satisfying decision-making practice? Kathy needed to give participants opportunities to practice each growth tool throughout the program. Then, they could brainstorm as a group how those growth tools could help people make more aligned decisions. Ideally, Kathy would set people up for success to leave the classroom feeling ready and confident to use new growth tools the next time they made a big decision in real life.

The answers to these questions revealed what Kathy should teach in her program. Instead of picking topics and introducing a new one every week—which is generally how educational curriculum is structured—she ended up strategically selecting content and activities based on how useful they were in supporting people to make decisions they felt good about.

Too often, instructional designers, trainers, teachers, and course creators identify what should be taught by selecting topics or subjects, but this leaves us with only face value learning. If we want to foster a deeper value of learning, we must first identify the value participants will get from the learning experience. To select what we should teach, we need to feature information and activities that address answers to all five components of the exercise. This approach is also excellent for helping us narrow down what content to include. It's easy to add everything plus the kitchen sink into your training programs, but doing so often overwhelms participants. This chapter introduces several core concepts to help you integrate instructional design, measurement, and evaluation to increase the TTV for individuals, organizations, and communities.

Confirm Behavior Change Actually Matters

Imagine you've just been asked to design a learning program. For example, your boss says she wants a team communication training because she's observed a high amount of conflict among teams recently. Or, a new client asks you to design a learning program to complement one of their recently published books. What do you do next? Conduct a needs assessment to explore the context of the training request? Ask your boss or your client the goal for the program? Ask your boss or client what they expect will change after participants complete the program?

This isn't a trick question. But it is a tricky one. The order in which you ask those questions is important because it will help you save time in the instructional design and evaluation processes that follow. Remember, there are two types of value gained from learning: face value and deeper value. You should first find out what value your boss or client expects from the requested training. The design and evaluation approach (and the corresponding time and resources you put into the program) will differ based on their answer.

I like to respond to requests for training with the third option—asking the requestor what they expect will change after participants complete the program. I like this question because it tells me what value they seek without asking, "Do you imagine this program having face value or deeper value?" For one thing, most folks are unlikely to know the difference between the face value and deeper value of learning. And, while most people want to create learning that has a deeper value for participants, they are only willing to invest in a program that disseminates information (face value). If you ask a question about change, it forces an alignment of expectations.

A dear colleague of mine, Chris Taylor, founder of Actionable.co, coaches all his clients to ask this question when a customer requests training: "Are you looking for someone to deliver training, or do you intend to have real change happen as a result of the program?" Essentially, does behavior change matter? If it does, you'll follow one design approach. If it doesn't, you'll follow another approach (one that's significantly less time consuming).

If you learn that behavior change matters, asking these two additional questions will help you gather information to prioritize the program content and measurement strategy:

- How are the behaviors you want to change aligned with strategic priorities for the individual, organization, or community?
- What is the fastest way to facilitate behavior change?

When a stakeholder asks for training, the first step is gathering information to find a solution that enables the desired outcome in the easiest, least time-consuming way. After all, training may not always be the best solution. The process of learning takes time. To increase the predictability that learning leads to the desired outcome, we must align multiple variables (recall that Cirque du Soleil–like precision I referenced at the beginning of this chapter). I first look to eliminate training and learning as a solution for the problem or opportunity at hand. Sometimes, a job aid, mentorship, performance support, coaching, or physical changes in the workplace environment will bring about change faster than a learning program.

If you learn that behavior change matters to the stakeholder, but they are only willing to give you two weeks (or some other short amount of time) to create the training solution, then you can have a conversation about their behavior change expectation. You could start by saying, "If you expect behavior and performance changes to come about from this program, I will need to invest more time to understand the problems and context contributing to the present performance situation. Additionally, I'll need to use a design approach that supports people truly changing their behavior, which is a combination of training and performance support. Is this something you are willing to invest in?" While having this type of conversation may be uncomfortable, once you have approval to invest in a needs assessment and training plus performance support, you are significantly more likely to offer a program that brings about real change (Binder 2017).

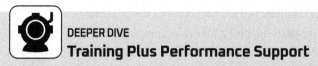

DEEPER DIVE
Training Plus Performance Support

If you're interested in a training plus performance support approach, read JD Dillon's 2022 book *The Modern Learning Ecosystem*. This book outlines useful performance support strategies that you can integrate into an organization's overall learning strategy.

Lead With Accomplishments Versus Subjects and Topics

Let's return to Kathy's story from the beginning of this chapter. She originally started her learning design process by identifying the most useful or insightful information (based on her own experience) and then organizing that information into a simple timeline. That's not a bad starting place to achieve a face value of learning. However, it won't lead to measurable behavior change outcomes and deeper-value learning.

The CEO of the Performance Thinking Network, Carl Binder (2017), who's known for his work in the areas of human performance technology and psychology, says that learning "interventions designed from beginning to end with a focus on valuable accomplishments are more effective, sustainable, and economical than those with other starting places in the analysis and design process."

The accomplishment-based curriculum design process, originally created by Joe Harless (1998), offers a different approach to determining what should be taught in education and training. Instead of identifying relevant subjects, topics, and skills, we should first identify the accomplishments (or outcomes) we want to achieve with our education initiatives. The accomplishments then determine what content and skills we should target.

Harless says, "An ounce of analysis up front might be worth a pound of interventions." With the right initial analysis, you can clarify the problem (or opportunity) your program is intended to influence along with the appropriate metrics to evaluate the program's success. Essentially, sourcing the right information up front should guide both the education and evaluation plan. Harless recommends using the following questions in your front-end analysis:

- What is the ultimate purpose and goal of the program?
- What should participants be able to accomplish after they engage in the program?
- What is the gap between current accomplishments and desired accomplishments?
- What are the root causes of this gap?
- What solutions or initiatives are best suited to solve the root causes?
- What content should be taught that supports solving the root causes?
- How should the educational experience be designed and delivered?
- What is the best way to evaluate if the program filled the gap between current and desired accomplishments?

DEEPER DIVE
The Accomplishment-Based Curriculum Process

Joe Harless tested his accomplishment-based curriculum process in a longitudinal study of two similar schools in Georgia. One designed a high school curriculum following the accomplishment-based approach, and the other followed the traditional subject-based approach. The school that followed the accomplishment-based approach saw a significant difference in key educational outcomes, such as higher attendance, college admission, and job acquisition rates. You can read more about his method and the study in his 1998 book *The Eden Conspiracy*.

Before embarking on the design and delivery of any initiative, you must clearly understand the gap between the current and desired accomplishments. You should know, without a doubt, the gap between what is and what should be. These questions are the perfect checks and balances to ensure that all critical components of an educational initiative are aligned, including the goal, the root cause, the content, and the evaluation strategy. Harless's questions also provide another approach (like the impact hypothesis) for outlining what you are doing and why.

The ultimate value of this front-end analysis is to work toward a Cirque du Soleil–like alignment of the factors that predictably increase your program's success. The questions aren't extensive and can be easily answered in a one-hour meeting. Ensure you get the necessary information from this strategic exploratory questioning by inviting your project's key stakeholders—including business stakeholders, end users, SMEs, and members of your team who are involved in the program's design, delivery, and management—to this meeting. Each stakeholder has a different perspective. If you don't invest time up front to collect each of their perspectives, you're less likely to design an aligned initiative.

Use Data Enablement to Track Real-Time Outcomes

One strategy of integrating measurement, evaluation, and instructional design is conducting a front-end analysis to source your content and evaluation strategies at one time. A second method of integrating instructional design with M&E is creating data-enabled learning programs. The data-enablement process is distinctly different from evidence-based or data-driven ones, and it can be easy to confuse these concepts. An evidence-based or data-driven curriculum, product, or program uses data that you've already collected and analyzed as evidence to support why and how you'll design and deliver your final product. Data enablement is the process of designing systems that collect original data while you facilitate your program. With this process, you get real-time insights while the program or product is being used, which you can leverage to create more reflective, deeper-value experiences and continuously adjust your approach to support participants in achieving the program's goals.

Data enablement doesn't have to be complex. It's simply a process of embedding data collection opportunities at strategic points throughout a program or curriculum to track participant progress and obtain feedback that you can apply immediately to improve the program and its outcomes. The trick to data enablement, especially for professionals working on a shoestring, is to invest a little more time up front to ensure the data collection methods provide information that is easy to summarize and analyze in real time. Data enablement won't help if you don't review the collected data until after the program is over, or worse yet, you use a collection method that leaves you with data that is cumbersome to review. Then, you likely won't use the data at all!

In the next few sections, we'll review some great examples of data enablement. I've either used the method myself or experienced it as a learner.

Kathy's Decision-Making Data-Enablement System

At the beginning of this chapter, I introduced you to Kathy's program. It was the perfect use case for data enablement. She crafted the learning experience around four core simulations. Each one introduced participants to a new growth tool that was designed to help them improve their decision-making skills. After every simulation, participants reflected on all the ways the growth tool could be useful in a decision-making scenario.

At the start of every workshop, participants answered a series of questions on how satisfied they were with any personal decisions they had made in the previous week, what influences guided their decisions, and what growth tools they specifically practiced using. This data was anonymously shared with participants as part of an icebreaker discussion. Participants attended 16 total workshops, which meant Kathy had 16 total data collection opportunities to see how people were progressing.

As a bonus, every participant received a growth report at the end of each new tool segment, as well as at the end of the complete learning experience. All data collection systems were built into the learning experience. She did not email surveys after the program was over, but collected data live within each workshop—automating data collection, analysis, and reporting. Thus, after she set up and tested the initial systems, she didn't need to do any further measurement and evaluation work. It took me and Kathy about 10 hours to set up her systems. Her program has been available to participants for more than two years now. The initial 10 hours of work gave her an infinite return on investment.

Dr. Pfifer's Writing Course Feedback Worksheet

Among the first few courses I took during my doctorate degree program was Dr. Pfifer's academic writing class. Many students (myself included) had little experience writing and publishing peer-reviewed journal articles. The goal of the course was to prepare us for writing a dissertation and publishing the research in one or more peer-reviewed journals. At the end of every class, Dr. Pfifer handed out a worksheet with three open-ended questions:

- After participating in this class, what concepts are you uncertain or unclear about?

- What unanswered questions do you have related to the content covered in today's class?
- What information, resources, or support do you think you still need to confidently write your literature review?

She put on some music and gave everyone three to five minutes to write down their answers. After every class, she read the worksheets and incorporated our feedback into the next class. This strategy did not involve technology. Instead, she crafted three simple questions, whose answers would give her useful feedback to support students in accomplishing the goal of the course (to write a literature review) and their doctorate program. She consistently read students' feedback and refined her curriculum as needed. This is data enablement at its finest!

Dan's Rose, Bud, Thorn Strategy

Let's now return to Dan's cohort course, which we discussed in chapter 3. One of the data-collection strategies he used was the rose, bud, thorn method, which I found to be incredibly thoughtful and useful. Dan offered six live workshops as part of the learning experience. Just like my academic writing professor, he asked people to share feedback on three things at the end of every one:

- **Rose**—what did you enjoy most in this workshop?
- **Bud**—what is something you are still thinking about, confused about, or want more information on?
- **Thorn**—what aspects of the workshop did you enjoy least and how might they be improved?

Unlike my academic writing professor, however, Dan collected this information digitally. He asked people to take a few minutes to complete the digital form. Dan then synced his survey data into one Google spreadsheet, which held all the data collected throughout the course showing feedback and growth from participants. This enabled Dan to easily look at a tab he named "Rose-Bud-Thorn" to see how participants' feedback evolved as the course unfolded, so he could adapt the learning experience accordingly.

Many people mistakenly think evaluation is something that only takes place after a learning experience, program, or project is over. This could not be further from the truth. Learning, progress, growth, and change are happening continuously throughout your program, and long after the program is over. Therefore, evaluation can and should be happening continuously as well. It's essential that we anticipate key growth milestones, capture data to show participants' progress, and collect feedback to support their unique needs.

A Shoestring Summary

The real benefit of using strategies shared in this chapter is saving time, which you can do by allocating resources appropriately in your learning design process (such as spending less time on face-value learning and more time on deeper-value learning). Participants save time if you've prioritized the content and activities in your learning experiences around essential practice and must-have information for behavior change (versus the kitchen sink approach of giving them more information than they need to know). Stakeholders reap the benefits of seeing growth outcomes immediately when you use a data-enabled approach to instructional design. If I've convinced you that these time-saving benefits are worth integrating into your existing approach, use the following action items to get started:

1. **Get clear.** Does change really matter? In the previous chapter, we addressed the measurement myth—we should measure and evaluate everything. You don't need to invest an equal amount of time, energy, and money into every program evaluation. Initiatives designed to facilitate change should receive a great deal of time and attention. Similarly, you don't need to invest an equal amount of time and resources in instructional design for initiatives that are not focused on change as the end goal.

2. **Find the gap between what is and what should be.** If you don't get the information you need after asking a supervisor or business leader, "What change do you expect to occur after participants complete a learning initiative?" try Joe Harless's accomplishment-based curriculum process for front-end analysis questions. What do you want participants to be able to accomplish after they complete your program? And, what is the gap between what's currently being

accomplished and what should be? Identifying this gap saves you time on instructional design and evaluation. It also informs the content of your curriculum and your metrics for evaluation. Why ask a series of questions when one can guide your education and evaluation plans?

3. **Practice data enablement.** If you aren't getting real-time data to understand your program's effectiveness—you should be! With technology advancements, it's easier than ever to set up systems (for free) to collect meaningful information that will help you better serve your customers, clients, and learners. How do you know if you're successfully practicing data enablement? You should be regularly using data to review, reflect, and perfect your programs. If you don't have data, or aren't using the data you have, it's time to improve your systems.

5

Evaluating and Improving Your Programs With New and Existing Data

In an ideal world, we start the learning design process by creating program outcomes and a strategy to calculate whether we've met our goals and targets. Essentially, we set ourselves up for success by collecting critical data before, during, and after the program to demonstrate its effectiveness. While this may be the ideal practice, it is not always a common practice. However, all hope is not lost for evaluating programs that didn't start with the end in mind.

So, should you invest resources to evaluate the outcomes of programs that didn't have a clear goal, or had a goal but no evaluation strategy? That depends on whether you want to use the data to improve future programs. Are you planning to facilitate the program again? Are you designing a similar one and want to explore successes and failures from the previous versions? Are you doing an audit of past programs and seek to understand patterns in engagement, participants' experiences, and performance changes to help improve your overall learning strategy? Each of these questions is an excellent use case for evaluating outcomes in the rearview mirror—borrowing available data to evaluate past programs.

If your boss or a client asks you to evaluate the outcomes of a program that didn't have a measurement strategy, but you aren't sure how to respond, start by asking these questions:

- Can you tell me what changes or outcomes you hoped or expected to see after participants completed the program?
- How do you plan to use the data from this program evaluation?

Your goal is to listen for evidence that your boss or client wants to use the data to improve the program (whether it's a new program or an existing one). You also want to know that they have a clear expected outcome. If you go into any measurement and evaluation project without a clear outcome, evaluation is nearly impossible. If your requestor says they didn't have any change expectations and simply want to know if the program was effective, take a deep breath. This statement is frustrating and contradictory. At this point, you should follow up by asking them to tell you what indicators to look for when you evaluate the program to determine if it was effective. If their answer still doesn't give you any criteria to investigate the program's effectiveness, then it's not worth your time or resources to conduct an evaluation. Your challenge now will be breaking this news to your boss or client.

In truth, most people (your boss and clients included) want to investigate the effects, outcomes, and results of learning to find out if it accomplished its goals. We want to know if the time and money we invested in our programs was worth it in the end. When tasked with evaluation in the rearview mirror, the primary mission is gathering data you can use to improve the program. Looking backward to evaluate a program that didn't have an original measurement strategy means you may not have a perfect dataset for demonstrating if the program was effective. However, you can find clues that you were moving in the right direction (or not). Rearview evaluation cases are successful when you have clear goals to investigate and you're able to find data (that's already been collected) to evaluate if the goals were achieved.

Looking in the Rearview Mirror to Increase Impact

After running several 12-week cohort courses, Nick and James, founders of a business development company specifically for real estate agents, noticed participant attendance rates and task completion were less than ideal. They also heard anecdotally that people were confused by some of the program components and wished there was a better organizing framework tying the learning experience together. Nick and James wanted to improve the program but had no idea where to begin.

To prioritize improvements for the program, they first needed to articulate what their cohort course made possible for each individual participant and for their business (their goals). In rearview evaluation cases, I appreciate using the language of possibilities to articulate goals: "What do you think will become possible for participants because they've completed your program?" and "What do you think is possible for your business because people are completing your program?" Nick and James thought participants would experience immediate business wins during and after the program. These wins could include referrals, network growth, new leads, and spending less time each week on lead generation. Their short-term business goal was generating revenue by selling more seats. Long-term, they sought customer retention— converting cohort-course customers into subscription-membership customers. Participants currently experienced the course as a one-and-done event. Nick and James wanted customers to experience their programs as a long-term source of support, helping to grow customers' businesses over time.

With clarity on the desired outcomes for customers and their business, I could help Nick and James explore what worked and what didn't in their past programs. We used a past program audit to identify strategies to bridge the gap between where they were and where they wanted to be. The exploration opened a pandoras box of data! When I asked where I could find data from their previous cohort courses, they gave me eight different types of data (Table 5-1).

Table 5-1. Data Sources From Nick and James's Past Program Audit

Data	Tech Platform
Participant registrations	Luma
Attendance	Zoom
Program intake survey	Typeform
Weekly wins report	Typeform
Weekly program feedback	Typeform
Activity completion	Todoist
Full cohort outcomes reports	Notion
Client testimonials	Airtable

To do a rearview past program audit, Nick and James would've needed to weed through all eight types from six different sources to discover themes from each cohort. Yikes! Luckily, Google Sheets naturally integrated with each of their tech platforms, so they were able to export their data into one master spreadsheet. This made the process much easier.

TIME SAVER

Integrating Your Data in One Place

If you're using multiple tech platforms to facilitate learning programs and monitor and evaluate their progress, finding a way to integrate the data into one source of truth will save you a lot of headaches when it's time to analyze your data. Google Sheets is a common option for integrating data from survey tools like Typeform, SurveyMonkey, and Jotform into one master source. It's as easy as switching on the Google Sheets integration for each survey or assessment tool you use. You can usually enter "integration" in the platform's help article's search bar to discover your integration options. If your company is a Salesforce or HubSpot user, these platforms are also common integration options.

Nick and James's impact hypothesis for their program was that if participants were exposed to their core business development theories and practiced several simple business development activities every week, then after 12 weeks, they would see a significant increase in business wins (such as network growth, referrals, and new leads). Thus, in my past program audit, I needed to look at week-over-week rates of completion (attendance and activity completion) and the week-over-week changes in business wins. I found that after six weeks, about 50 percent of the cohort stopped showing up and only about a third of the group was doing their weekly business development activities. I also found that the people who showed up to weekly workshops and completed the business development activities were more likely to report business wins every week. Effectively, if Nick and James could increase engagement in the program, they could improve the program outcomes. I then looked to the qualitative feedback data to explore what was contributing to decreased engagement after week 6. In the end, there were three clear opportunities to improve engagement rates:

- Shorten the course to six weeks by reorganizing the program around six critical business development activities instead of 12 business development theories. (Does this sound familiar? It's the same major change I made with Kathy's decision-making course. There is so much gained by organizing learning programs around the critical practices that drive the desired accomplishments, rather than organizing by topic).
- Add weekly group working sessions with a coach to help participants practice and troubleshoot, and to encourage them to complete their weekly business development tasks.
- Simplify the task completion data-collection process by incorporating check-ins and sharing wins at the start of every live workshop. Previously, Nick and James were sending email and text reminders asking participants to check "complete" on their Todoist activity list. Now, they were using the same Typeform every week for people to input their data and anonymously sharing results live with the whole cohort. Participants greatly enjoyed seeing the growth in business wins week over week. This encouraged everyone to input their data and share what worked and what didn't openly in a live discussion.

After implementing these changes, Nick and James saw a 75 percent average weekly workshop attendance rate, 60 percent task completion rate, and significant increases in business wins between week 1 and week 6 for nearly 100 percent of participants. They achieved an impressive change in impact by using insights from a rearview past program audit.

Data artifacts live everywhere and not just in a digital format. We operate in business environments that are swimming in data. The challenge we face is likely not a lack of data. In fact, your organization is collecting information on employees, students, and customers all the time (maybe without you even recognizing how much information you have at your disposal). The true challenge is knowing what data is most useful, getting access to it, and then analyzing it. Nick and James didn't have any formal evaluation strategies in place to show if they were accomplishing their goals. I'm not advocating that you forego creating a thoughtful evaluation plan as you design learning programs. However, if you did not create a specific evaluation strategy and still want to explore program outcomes, you likely have some data available to help you understand if your program hit or missed the mark. And more importantly, find opportunities to improve impact.

Use Clear Criteria to Select the Most Relevant Data

The downside of operating in business environments rich in data is figuring out the most relevant data for your evaluation needs. Creating clear criteria will help you save time during data collection and analysis. I'd like to take you down a rabbit hole for just a moment to show how important and time saving it is to outline specific criteria.

When I'm not doing measurement and evaluation work, you can find me renovating houses. Doing home improvement projects is a nice way to balance the highly analytical, cognitive-heavy work of learning design and M&E. When I first started home renovations, it was difficult to find the perfect investment property. There were many houses to review weekly on the multiple listing service (MLS). I spent hours with my realtor driving around town and looking at more houses than I probably should have. My first home renovation project required a bathroom addition. It was more costly than I originally imagined and difficult and time consuming to work within the permitting process. Also, because I was adding onto an older home, I ran into some unexpected expensive surprises. That's when my first criteria were born. I decided that my next investment property would have to be in a specific neighborhood and have a minimum of two bathrooms, a detached garage, zoning for two or three dwelling units, no foundation issues, and only one major structural problem (such as a leaking roof, old HVAC system, or plumbing concerns). Can you imagine what happened when I started looking for my next property? With criteria clearly communicated to my realtor, I saved time when looking at properties online and in person. Both my realtor and I were happier.

So, what should your criteria be when you take on a rearview evaluation project? It will be shaped by the following information:

- **Time specific.** This one is the easiest. What date range should your data artifacts be from?

- **Target population.** This could be as simple as "people who completed any leadership development program in the last 12 months," or as specific as "new managers internally promoted to roles serving the sales team in the year 2023."
- **Outcomes explored.** These are the hoped for or expected results of the training program. If you don't know what they are, ask your stakeholders the two questions we discussed at the beginning of this chapter. If they don't give you any clear outcomes, then a rearview evaluation is simply not possible.

Once you know what you're looking for, it's time to explore where to find these data artifacts. To do this, ask yourself, "Where can I find information on [*insert outcomes*]?" You can also get your team or a group of colleagues together to work this out.

Data artifacts are everywhere. They don't necessarily live in your LMS or LXP. Sometimes, we need to think outside the tech stack to brainstorm the variety of data we have access to. Consider an example. Let's say you want to evaluate changes in employee engagement. You might write on a whiteboard all the places you can think of where data on employee engagement could be found, such as:

- Company-wide meeting attendance
- Slack conversations
- Responses to employee feedback surveys
- Feedback in exit surveys
- Views or clicks on documents in an employee resource portal
- Participation in a volunteer mentorship program
- Ratio of tenured versus new employee attendance at monthly new employee happy hours

Don't hold back in this brainstorming session. More ideas equate to more options when selecting relevant data points for evaluation. However, not all data points revealed in a brainstorming session will be useful for your evaluation project. Thus, you'll want to select the artifacts that are realistically aligned with both the content in the training program and the program outcomes. For example, say you are evaluating an onboarding program featuring content about organizational culture and values like collaboration and connectedness. And perhaps the program's call to action was to engage in company-wide meetings and new employee happy hours and regularly share suggestions for improving the workplace environment. In this case, you could select data artifacts that are aligned with this content and the outcome of increased employee engagement, or a targeted rate of employees who are engaged. You might select these four data points:

1. Company-wide meeting attendance
2. Response rate of employee feedback surveys
3. Feedback in employee feedback surveys
4. Ratio of tenured versus new employee attendance at monthly new employee happy hours

Measurement is not always easy, but that doesn't mean it's not possible. The challenge is reframing what seems to be impossible (especially if technology limits how easy or intuitive measurement is) into something possible. Often, this means stepping outside the technology environment. The beauty is that you can always find data artifacts to monitor your targeted change. Once you do, you can leverage technology in its highest and best use: automating and managing administrative tasks to help you translate manual data collection and analysis into an automated process. (More on this topic in chapter 8.)

Improve the Integrity of Rearview Evaluation by Reducing Bias

While operating in a data rich environment makes rearview evaluation possible, using data that was not collected for the express purpose of evaluating your learning program can lead to biased evaluation. The saying "garbage in, garbage out" applies here. If you're using data collected for some other purpose, double-check that it is appropriate for your rearview evaluation use case. For example, let's say you're exploring outcomes for a leadership development program facilitated with a group of new managers who identify as women. You assert that participants will have higher rates of promotion and retention compared with new managers who didn't complete the leadership development program. You discover that HR collects data on internal promotions and employee retention. However, your HR manager is only able to give you this data for employees of all genders. Will this bias the outcomes of your rearview evaluation? Indeed, it will.

Comparing rates of promotion and retention for women who completed your leadership program with new managers of all genders who did not complete the program, it's possible you'd discover that program participants were promoted at a lower rate than the all-gender group. To reduce bias, you would need to isolate women managers from the promotion and retention dataset, which would allow you to compare outcomes from a target population that shared similar qualities. In this case, gender identity is the shared quality.

There are many other qualities that could influence outcomes in addition to gender, such as prior experience, being a native English speaker, or having a close friend or relative in a supervisory role within the organization. But I don't want to overwhelm you with the numerous ways data can be biased. It is important to recognize the limitations of working with secondary data—or datasets collected by others for their own unique purposes. Working with secondary data can be an extreme time saver because you'll save the time it would have taken you to collect the data yourself. However, you need to consider the characteristics of the dataset and determine if the secondary data sample aligns with the qualities and characteristics of the target population you are researching.

To reduce bias in your rearview evaluation projects, validating that you're working with an appropriate dataset is an important first step. In my work with Nick and James, this was easy because the data we used in the past program audit came from participants who completed their cohort course. We weren't comparing outcomes between participants who completed Nick and James's programs and a competitor's business development program. Had this been the case, we would have had to compare outcomes across a variety of learner characteristics, such as length of time as a business owner, size of business, gender, geographic location, reason for joining the program, and specialty. Any one of these variables could significantly influence the outcomes participants received from the program. In addition to validating you're working with the most appropriate datasets, there are two additional bias-reducing strategies that are regularly used in academic research: data triangulation and control groups. Incorporating these strategies into your rearview mirror evaluation requires very little additional time or resources but goes a long way to ensure the outcomes of your evaluation project are valid.

We dove into data triangulation in chapter 3. I want to emphasize how important triangulation is in the context of working with secondary datasets.

Triangulation can be done using mixed research methods (quantitative and qualitative), varying your data sources, or leveraging multiple theories to test your research hypotheses (Alele and Malau-Aduli 2023). For professionals working on a shoestring, varying your data sources will be the most accessible, time- and cost-effective way of leveraging data triangulation. Return to the four data artifacts to evaluate the example onboarding program (company-wide meeting attendance, response rate of employee feedback surveys, feedback in employee feedback surveys, and ratio of tenured versus new employee attendance at monthly new employee happy hours). Will those four data points give you the benefits of triangulation?

Yes. Of the four data points, at least one is qualitative. Thus, they don't all offer numerical data. Next, they represent four different data sources: One is learning activity data (attendance rates), one is self-reported data (survey responses), another is qualitative narrative feedback, and the last is a ratio of new versus tenured employee attendance. If you only used data points from self-reported surveys to evaluate in the rearview mirror, you wouldn't receive the benefits of triangulation that come from a more diverse dataset.

The next research strategy to help you preserve the integrity of your rearview evaluation is a control group. Using control groups simply means comparing one group of people who participated in a learning initiative with a similar group that did not participate. (Don't confuse control groups with the randomized controlled trials you commonly hear about in pharmaceutical drug studies. While randomized controlled trials are important for identifying, monitoring, and evaluating any potential harmful outcomes of new drugs or other health interventions, they are very resource heavy.)

Using control groups is an easy way to increase the credibility of your rearview evaluation projects. The trick to using this method is that you have enough longitudinal data on both groups—the control group (those who did not complete training) and the intervention group (those who did complete training). Let's say that the example onboarding program was voluntary, or it was being implemented in certain regions but not in others. That would give you excellent control groups. You could compare employee engagement data among people who voluntarily participated in the onboarding program versus those who did not, or you could compare employee engagement data among regions that implemented onboarding versus those that did not.

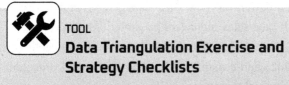

TOOL
Data Triangulation Exercise and Strategy Checklists

Use the data triangulation exercise in the appendix to check if your dataset meets the basic requirements of triangulation. You'll also find some strategy checklists for using data triangulation.

Remember, there are only two types of data: *narratives* and *numbers*. In research terms, they are *categorical* and *numerical* data. In research methodology, they are *qualitative* (research providing narrative data) and *quantitative* data (research providing numerical data). One easy way to increase the validity of your data collection efforts is to use both numerical and narrative data to investigate the same outcome. If both datasets tell a similar story of outcomes and impact, you can have more confidence that the story is valid and trustworthy.

Recall the case study I shared in chapter 3 about Larry Mohl. He wanted to use self-reported data to evaluate changes in inclusivity. He incorporated both quantitative and qualitative research questions in his assessment tool and compared the results from both datasets. Did they tell a similar story? If so, he could be confident his outcomes had a higher level of validity.

Additionally, remember the last time you wrote an essay or literature review as an assignment for a class? Do you remember completing your references list? A references list is a great way of thinking about data sources. To triangulate data for the purposes of reducing bias and increasing the validity of your outcomes, vary your sources.

Control groups won't perfectly eliminate bias. There will always be other factors that might be more influential than participating in training. For example, if regions where an organization does not offer onboarding have more formal cultures or hierarchical leadership, employee engagement might look very different. And that will have nothing to do with the presence or lack of training. Thus, if you are using control groups to increase the integrity of your rearview mirror evaluation, ensure you are using a large enough sample size—or about 10 percent of the total possible population (Conroy 2018). So, let's say your target population was new sales managers promoted internally in 2023 compared with new sales managers promoted internally in 2022. If there were 100 new managers in 2023 and 80 in 2022, you should collect data from 10 managers in 2023 and 8 managers in 2022. This would represent 10 percent of the respective total target populations.

There will be times when control groups are simply not possible. Returning to the example onboarding program, imagine that in the last five years all employees participated in the same onboarding program. In that case, you wouldn't have a relevant control group to use. In my rearview evaluation work with Nick and James, we also didn't have a control group, because we only had access to data from participants who were enrolled in the program. In these cases, you can use time as a variable to help increase the integrity of data analysis. We had five or more cohorts to compare data points and participant's qualitative feedback. Thus, themes that came up consistently throughout all five cohorts would have the most weight in that rearview evaluation.

Integrate Your Data Sources Into One Location

ATD Research reports from 2009, 2016, and 2023, as well as a 2022 report from Watershed all reveal another common challenge to measuring learning outcomes (whether in the rearview or from the beginning)—data is difficult to access. There are likely two reasons for this: a gatekeeper problem and a lack of integration. Let's address the integration problem first, as despite popular belief, navigating the gatekeeper problem is quite easy.

In Nick and James's shoestring success story, their rearview evaluation project involved data from eight different sources across five courses. That is a huge amount of data! And of course, it wasn't all funneled into one source. Before integrating the data, I helped Nick and James select the most relevant dataset. Effectively, we cut the total from eight sources to five (Table 5-2).

Two integrate all the data sources into one central location (where I could do the rearview analysis), I needed to identify the most appropriate data hosting tool to send all these sources to. The most common places to host data are:

- Microsoft Excel
- Google Sheets

- Customer relationship management (CRM) platforms
- Learning record stores (LRS)
- Human resource management (HRM) platforms

Table 5-2. Focused List of Data Sources

Data	Tech Platform
~~Participant registrations~~	~~Luma~~
Attendance	Zoom
~~Program intake survey~~	~~Typeform~~
Weekly wins report	Typeform
Weekly program feedback	Typeform
Activity completion	Todoist
Full cohort outcomes reports	Notion
~~Client testimonials~~	~~Airtable~~

Microsoft Excel and Google Sheets are the more cost effective and simpler tools to use. However, most organizations also have a CRM system that stores data about employees, customers, transactions, business leads, and marketing activities. The most popular CRM platforms over the last 15 years, largely because of their integration capability, are Salesforce and HubSpot. Nearly any type of data you can imagine can be either directly input or transferred from another platform and then stored in these systems. Sophisticated CRM tools have incredible reporting and data visualization capabilities too.

LRSs offer a different type of data hosting. They can extract any data artifact from any platform you use to deliver learning content and experiences to employees, students, or customers. Like with Salesforce and HubSpot, you'll need to select a specific LRS vendor to get the benefits of data integration. LRS vendors don't come cheap; however, organizations working with immense amounts of data, who don't already have a CRM, will find that acquiring an LRS with great data reporting and visualization features is an important investment to understand business outcomes associated with training and performance support programs.

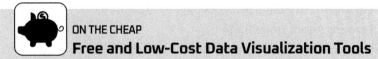

ON THE CHEAP
Free and Low-Cost Data Visualization Tools

If you are using Microsoft Excel or Google Sheets to collect and store your data, you'll likely need to use another platform to visualize it to tell stories about outcomes and impact. Both programs have native analytics functionality and visualization tools that can get you started without breaking the bank.

So, what is the most appropriate data hosting tool for integrating your data into one location? If your organization or client doesn't have a CRM, or isn't using it at a high level, then consider one of the simpler solutions. In Nick and James's case, they had a CRM, but they only used it to track customer payments, addresses, and phone numbers. They weren't planning to use any artifacts in their CRM for the rearview evaluation. We then looked at all integration options within the available data sources (Zoom, Typeform, Todoist, and Notion) by searching each platform's website to find the list of other platforms they could integrate with.

Google Sheets integrated with all of Nick and James's digital data sources. So, I created one Google spreadsheet; then, I turned on Google Sheets integration and added my new spreadsheet as the location for each source to send its data to. Now, all the data would magically appear in one place and Nick, James, and I could finally analyze it.

Getting Help Analyzing Data

Even for a data nerd like me, data analysis can be overwhelming. When I have the budget, I often contract data analysis out to someone who is faster and more experienced. (Chapter 7 includes advice for determining when it's best to hire external contractors versus building expertise yourself.) Most professionals working on a shoestring will likely be the data collector, analyzer, and storyteller for any evaluation project. I've been in this position many times too! There are four things I suggest you do to make this process less painful.

1. Write Down the Story You Hope to Tell With Your Data Before Analyzing It

The process of analyzing data means that you need to know mathematically how to calculate the numbers. For most L&D professionals, math isn't a favorite subject. Luckily, the mathematical equations necessary for learning outcome evaluations won't often require a highly complex statistical analysis. Sums, averages, and ratios are the equations you'll most frequently work with. You don't even have to calculate the numbers yourself. You simply need to tell Microsoft Excel or Google Sheets what formula to use.

For example, in my work with Nick and James, our hypothesis was that if people engaged in 75 percent or more of the program, they would see growth in new business leads as a result. For all five cohorts, we calculated the following averages for every week:

- Attendance rate
- Task-completion rate
- Business wins

We then plotted those numbers on a scatter plot to determine how all averages compared week over week and cohort over cohort. In this scatter plot, we could see the attendance rates drop off at six weeks and the consistently low task-completion rate every week. We also created a scatter plot of participants with low task-completion rates compared with high task-completion rates to find out if there was a strong relationship between task-completion rate and business wins. And there was!

2. Partner With Data and Technology Experts in Your Organization

L&D professionals often feel alone—as if they're on an island. And L&D professionals working on a shoestring often wear all the hats associated with driving the learning function in their organizations. When working with data, we don't need to build sophisticated analysis skill sets. We simply need to get comfortable asking for help. Nearly every organization, large enterprise, government agency, nonprofit, and small- or medium-sized business has at least one person (if not a whole team) devoted to IT, data management, and business intelligence. You will want to become friends and partners with these folks. What software tools does your organization already use to manage large datasets? What data analysis and visualization tools are business intelligence staff using? Who can help you translate your data from a spreadsheet to a report of outcomes and impact? All these questions can likely be answered by employees who you may not regularly work with—the people in IT and data management. Bring your impact hypothesis and the data you've collected to them, and you may be pleasantly surprised at the analysis and visualization support you'll find.

3. Invest Time Learning How to Use Pivot Tables

The digital era has brought the gift of YouTube. I cannot tell you how many things I've taught myself how to do thanks to YouTube. I installed my first sink with the help of YouTube videos, and I've learned how to use countless Microsoft Excel formulas and conditions to calculate learning outcomes. Once you know the story you want to tell with your data and you've determined the mathematical formulas (such as average, sum, or ratio) necessary for testing your impact story, you'll need to visualize the data.

The scatter plots I created with Nick and James were all made possible by pivot tables. Pivot tables use data from cells throughout all the worksheets in a spreadsheet to visualize relationships between core variables. I taught myself how to use Google Sheets with the help of Google tutorials, YouTube, and recently ChatGPT. Every time I encountered a challenge with a formula or function, I found an answer online—the key is knowing what calculations and comparisons you want to explore within your dataset. Using the right key words will help you get to the right resources. Some keywords include *pivot tables* (of course), *data analysis, summary worksheets*, and any specific formulas or mathematical calculations you're working with. Making time to learn and practice creating pivot tables may be the skill that seals the deal on your next promotion!

4. Use Generative AI Language Learning Models (LLMs) to Analyze Your Dataset

Generative artificial intelligence (AI) technology is evolving so rapidly, I shudder to think about reading this paragraph three months from now. Currently, the leading LLMs on the market are GPT-3.5, GPT-4, Gemini (formerly known as Bard), Cohere, PaLM, and Claude. These tools have the capability to analyze data from uploaded documents. If you use clear prompts, you can get assistance with data analysis (more on prompting best practices in chapter 8). As with any tool used to create reports or analyze data, you must create a clear hypothesis to test and write clear investigative questions.

I've referenced the phrase "garbage in, garbage out" a few times, and it's applicable when using generative AI to analyze a dataset. Once you have all your data integrated into one spreadsheet, you can use your generative AI tool of choice and ask questions like, "What is the average week one attendance rate for all five courses?" With extremely clear questions (and a clean dataset), generative AI can take some of the complexity out of the analysis. It will take some practice to refine your prompt and question technique, but digital tools that incorporate AI will only continue to blossom and be ingrained in your regular workflows. Don't be afraid to test these tools and capabilities out. The more practice you have working with AI, the sooner you can enjoy its sophistication and time saving benefits. But remember, while AI is smart, it's not always right. Until you've used an AI tool consistently enough to test its reliability, always have someone (that new friend in IT perhaps) check your work!

Get Past the Data Gatekeeper

A colleague recently complained to me that her HR director would not grant her access to exit survey data, no questions asked. I didn't want to fuel her frustration by asking for more details about how she approached them with the data request, but I suspect her director lacked a compelling reason for sharing the survey data and was likely concerned with data privacy and permissions. In my experience, the data gatekeeper problem often comes down to three root causes:

- Lack of a clear and compelling reason for requesting the data
- Lack of a strategy explaining how the data will help the business (not just the learning department)
- Existing policies and procedures around data privacy and protection

You can get past the data gatekeeper with a clear vision and creative problem solving. First, you should present a clear hypothesis of how your learning initiative is intended to contribute to short- or long-term business outcomes. Then, show all the data you'll be collecting to prove your hypothesis and how your data request fits into the overall vision. This strategy offers a clear and compelling reason and proves to the gatekeeper your intention is to be of greater service to the business.

If your vision and compelling reason doesn't move the gatekeeper into a resounding yes, your challenge is likely a data permissions and privacy issue. In that case, you may be asking the wrong person for access to data. Data gatekeepers are frequently very good at upholding policies and procedures, which is part of their job description. You need to uncover the right person to ask for data access, or under what conditions you may be able to use the data. For example, the data may simply need to be scrubbed of any personal identifying information.

In the next chapter, we dive into getting buy-in from stakeholders and nurturing strategic and fulfilling partnerships with a few key allies in your organization. If the data gatekeepers cannot help you due to data permission and privacy policies, it's time to carefully move up stream. Building relationships with key decision makers in your organization is an important part of doing great evaluation work. You don't need to have relationships with all leaders; you simply need start with one ally (ideally in operations) with whom you can build a mutually supportive partnership. Sharing your vision of how the learning function and learning activities are designed to increase operational success with decision makers may be just the antidote to your gatekeeper problem.

A Shoestring Summary

Operating in a fast-paced environment, where things change regularly, with limited access to data (at least for now) creates a tough context for us to evaluate learning. This is true whether we are working on a shoestring or not. The action items listed here are small simple steps that will help you stay focused, invest your time wisely, and not let less than ideal situations prevent you from your measurement and evaluation goals:

1. **Confirm rearview evaluation is a worthy investment.** What do you plan to do with the data, insights, or outcomes of your evaluation work? Measurement and evaluation are investments of time and

resources. If you've been asked to evaluate a program that did not have an evaluation strategy already in place, clarify first what the requestor plans to do with the data gleaned from your evaluation work. Estimate how much time it will take you, what tools you need to use, and how much of other people's time it will require. Then, translate that into a dollar amount and ask the requestor if that dollar amount is a worthy investment to get the outcomes they seek.

2. **Select clear criteria to guide your rearview evaluation project.** Once you've confirmed the rearview evaluation project is a worthy investment, ensure you're selecting the best data using these criteria: specific time, focused target population, and clear outcomes for your investigation.

3. **Implement bias reducing strategies in your rearview evaluation work.** All research and evaluation work has some bias. Your goal is not to remove it completely, but to increase the trustworthiness of your outcomes. How can you increase the confidence that the outcomes you've discovered are valid? Use appropriate datasets, data triangulation, and control groups.

4. **Integrate data into one source of truth.** Most organizations use numerous physical and digital platforms to manage day-to-day operations. This means there are many sources of data living in different departments and physical locations across the organization. For this data to be useful, datasets must be able communicate with one another. Luckily, many technology platforms have native integration options that allow you to push and pull data from one digital location to another (once they're turned on). In other cases, your data must be manually moved into your preferred source of truth (such as a CRM, data hosting software, or LRS). Determine the best place for all the data to live, and then make a checklist of all the integration activities that you must do to get the data into this final location for analysis.

5. **Ask for help with any of the data collection, integration, or analysis activities you aren't comfortable with.** Whether you're a consultant, vendor, or internal L&D professional, you've probably experienced moments of frustration when you simply didn't have

the knowledge, skills, or time to facilitate one (or many) parts of the M&E equation. In these cases, you must ask for help. You could find the nearest IT staff member in your organization, tell them what you want to do with data you've collected, and ask what tools the organization has access to that may help. Or, you could reach out on LinkedIn to learning communities and ask what strategies or tech solutions they've found valuable. Or, you could consult Google or YouTube for tutorials instead of aimlessly trying to navigate Microsoft Excel or any other tool you aren't familiar with.

PART III
BUY

Much of measurement and evaluation on a shoestring comes down to strategic and critical thinking. In the first two parts of this book, you discovered that there is a lot you can do to show program outcomes without buying anything! Yet, there are also support resources, tools, and technology that, when invested wisely, can give you truly remarkable returns.

Everything from program design to measurement and evaluation is easier when you have stakeholder buy-in. Thus, a book for shoestring professionals is incomplete without suggestions for how to build strong partnerships with all stakeholders and beneficiaries of your programs. Automation and AI are also essential sources of time-saving support. Because we live in a world of big data, we must be prepared for making informed decisions on when and how to buy technology tools. With the right strategies and a little critical thinking, you can build, borrow, and buy—even on a shoestring budget.

In this part of the book, you'll explore how to:

- Apply best practices for getting buy-in and facilitating mutually beneficial relationships with all stakeholders of your programs.
- Decide when it's best to buy external support from consultants, contractors, and vendors versus building a viable solution yourself.
- Leverage automation and AI smartly, safely, and efficiently.

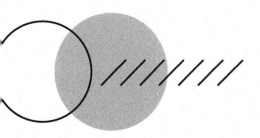

6

Getting Buy-In and Measuring Impact Without the Ideal Support System

What will it take for learning and business leaders to align? In most organizations, it seems the learning function is the only business unit (compared with marketing, product, operations, sales, and service) that remains elusively disconnected from a business's KPIs. Why is this so and how do we solve this historical challenge?

We all find ourselves in situations with less-than-ideal stakeholder support. If we don't build a stable partnership with key stakeholders, we may always be fighting for resources and support to do our jobs well. Making learning stick, transfer, or predictably translate into new actions, capabilities, or habits requires a supportive environment. Social support (provided by training facilitators, peers, and organizational leaders) to check in on learners' progress and reinforce expected behavior changes after a training program is over can increase the likelihood of change by up to 34 percent (Actionable.co 2022). Additionally, when training facilitators simply check in, either digitally or in-person, a few times after training, these touchpoints help make behavior change stick. Can you imagine what impact might be possible if training facilitators, peers, managers, and organizational leaders all worked together to support a learning initiative?

Getting Buy-In From the Ground Up

After working in public health education for nearly five years, I decided it was time for a new challenge. I accepted a leadership position in a new industry within an entirely different type of organization. The first year was the honeymoon phase. Working closely with my supervisor, I prioritized the training department's initiatives that aligned with pressing and pervasive performance and operations challenges. For a while, the initiatives hit their completion and performance targets, but then everything changed. The organization received a huge influx of money, moved into a new building, added 25 percent more staff, and restructured senior leadership roles and responsibilities. Goals and expectations changed seemingly overnight, and everyone (from entry-level employees to C-suite executives) struggled to keep up.

With this immense change happening in such a short period, communication became the main source of performance challenges in the organization. While the changes being implemented were necessary for growth and had the potential to help the organization fulfill its mission in exciting, new ways, the unintended consequence (lack of communication) came at a terrible time. My department needed to renew an application for our primary source of funding, which required clear and compelling data demonstrating that the organization was operating efficiently and hitting its minimum service and performance goals. (It was not!)

To do my job well, I needed to consistently know what was happening with frontline employees, managers, technology partners, and operations staff. As the training director, I was one of few employees who had regular touchpoints with nearly every department in the organization. I needed good data, and I needed it fast. With the restructuring taking place, and the operations team focused on a smooth transition into a new building, I decided to forgo asking for permission to take on a data collection project. Instead, I leveraged the relationships I'd built with staff across departments and got to work putting puzzle pieces together to understand the organization's current performance on key grant deliverables.

This project was important for me for two reasons. First, in this organization, training was historically seen as the silver bullet for performance problems. As a result, if training did not solve performance gaps, the training department was usually blamed. I knew training wasn't the solution for all performance challenges and I wanted data to prove it. Second, I wanted a system to determine if our training programs were effective. This project offered a feedback loop to help me continuously prioritize updates to our programs and develop new solutions.

The organization's KPIs were synonymous with its grant deliverables, which were accessible in the grant application stored on the organization's intranet. I wrote each grant deliverable (service and performance target) on a sticky note and placed them randomly on a whiteboard. Then, I mapped the relationship between the training, performance, operations, and service deliverables. I linked all the deliverables into a story that demonstrated how training could positively influence the organization's service goals. The result looked unsurprisingly like the hypothesis framework I described in chapter 2.

By completing this mapping exercise, I discovered an interesting relationship among all the deliverables: Managers were central to monitoring and communicating progress and problems for each one. They were the essential provider of the data I needed to see the interconnectedness of training, employee performance, operations, and services. Managers were required to listen in on live conversations between employees and clients every week. They completed a standard report with every observation, which documented strengths, areas for improvement, and any observed technology problems. What do you imagine the organization did with these reports? Nothing!

The grant manager was tasked with reviewing the reports and inputting scores for each employee into a comprehensive spreadsheet. She was among few staff members who knew that cumulative data was available. I scheduled a meeting with her, showed her my sticky noted whiteboard, and shared my concerns about organizational blind spots in understanding opportunities to improve training and operations. Would she be willing to share the data with me, the managers, and the operations team? In our meeting, I learned that because the grant manager had so many other responsibilities, she was often months behind transferring this data onto the comprehensive spreadsheet. So, I asked if our new training coordinator could help, because she had extra time and needed to learn more about our services and operations.

My quest to find good data to better understand the organization's baseline performance on grant deliverables and identify opportunities for improvement revealed an understaffing problem. Because manager report data was essential to the training and operations functions, the training coordinator and the lead frontline staff manager allocated 25 percent of their weekly work hours to transferring data. Over time, the organization invested in technology systems to automate most of the data management process. In the end, I created a system offering continuous feedback so training and operations could see real-time opportunities to bridge gaps in performance and service. You can imagine how this continuous feedback loop helped me gain trust and build meaningful partnerships with my organization's stakeholders. Through this initiative, I proved that I was just as invested in operational success as they were. With these partnerships in place, it was easier for me to gain buy-in for future initiatives.

The success of my shoestring story was possible because I was confident taking the initiative to explore possible solutions to my organization's performance and service gaps, even without having the authority to do so. Confidence and agency are essential to doing the work that will equip your function and the business for long-term success. You must be tenacious and dedicated to building this agency. You will be pleasantly surprised by how stakeholder relationships evolve as a result.

Build Relationships With Colleagues Throughout Your Organization

What I didn't mention in the previous story is that I entered my leadership role as an outsider when historically my position had been filled from within. You can imagine the resistance I experienced from colleagues as an outsider newly charged with leading the training department. I quickly learned that this organization's culture prioritized the frontline workers' needs and perspectives. After all, their dedicated performance enabled the organization to provide 24-hour service nationally. I also learned that the frontline staff had significant influence and was, at times, directly engaged with nearly all departments and many stakeholders in the organization. Training was no exception. For the training function (and my position as an outsider) to be effective, I needed solid relationships with frontline staff.

To build relationships, I leveraged coffee breaks. I would leave my desk two to three times per day, fill my empty coffee mug, and walk the floor. In the beginning of my tenure, I just observed. People weren't overly friendly at first.

I accepted that it would take time to build trust and rapport. I intentionally chose different times of day to take my coffee breaks so I'd get face time with staff across different shifts. Eventually, I felt comfortable asking them questions about their work—careful not to take too much time away from their required duties. Managers (whose offices were scattered throughout the floor) started to take notice of my coffee breaks. In time, they asked me to step into their offices. They'd share insights with me about challenges their team members faced and ask for my opinion. Then one day, my supervisor asked me to step into his office and shared, "Alaina, managers are telling me how much they appreciate you getting to know the frontline staff. I appreciate you taking the initiative to do this."

During my time at this organization, I grew from a department of one to a department of three. I hired an outsider and insider. The success of my coffee chats led me to institute an onboarding practice that required any new member of the training team (especially outsiders) to spend a certain amount of time shadowing frontline staff, going through the same training as frontline staff, and even taking a certain number of calls (just like a frontline staff member). As the department leader, I too stepped into this role on a semiregular basis. It was essential to keep a pulse on the frontline work experience so my department could be proactive in supporting ongoing staff needs (training or otherwise).

The relationships I created with the frontline staff (the life blood of the organization) had a trickle up effect. Staff and managers readily shared their praise with upper management once they saw the genuine commitment and care of the training department. Instead of working hard to obtain buy-in and build relationships from the top town, I prioritized relationships with the people the organization valued most—the frontline staff. They became the learning team's greatest advocates. These relationships made it possible to have regular touchpoints with managers in multiple departments. I didn't come by only when there was a problem or I needed something. My touchpoints were also simply friendly one-off conversations sharing good news or the weekend's happenings, or answering questions related to training. I never took much time, just enough to maintain collaborative and supportive relationships to ultimately support projects like the one I shared at the start of this chapter.

Discover the Core Metrics Driving Your Organization

One of the easiest ways to lose a stakeholder's trust is to throw up your hands in the face of constant change and say, "Showing outcomes of my work is too difficult because you keep moving the goal post." Trust me. Business leaders only move goal posts preemptively or in reaction to their own goal posts being moved. Change is hard for everyone. It's also inevitable. Remember that business leaders are charged with gaining or maintaining competitive advantage in the marketplace and generating revenue to preserve viability—and your job! That is a lot of pressure.

Many learning leaders argue that L&D professionals must think of themselves as a business unit and take accountability for speaking the language of the business. Seeing yourself as a business unit first and a learning unit second and speaking the language of business fluently gives you the key ingredient to be successful in the face of change. We need a clear understanding of the core metrics driving our organizations, and it's not always profit. This is especially true in nonprofits, government agencies, education institutions, and healthcare companies. We could also argue that profit is not the only driving force in for-profit organizations. While revenue and expenses matter for all types of organizations, core metrics driving a business will never be limited to profit alone.

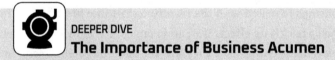

DEEPER DIVE
The Importance of Business Acumen

Check out these excellent resources that clearly document why it's important for learning professionals to build their business acumen:

- Dana Gaines Robinson, James C. Robinson, Jack J. Phillips, Patricia Pulliam Phillips, and Dick Handshaw, *Performance Consulting: A Strategic Process to Improve, Measure, and Sustain Organizational Results*, 3rd ed. (Oakland, CA: Berrett-Koehler Publishers, 2015).
- Ingrid Guerra-López and Karen Hicks, *Partner for Performance: Strategically Aligning Learning and Development* (Alexandria, VA: ATD Press, 2017).
- Kristopher Newbauer, *Aligning Instructional Design With Business Goals: Make the Case and Deliver Results* (Alexandria, VA: ATD Press, 2023).

So, if profit is not the core metric to focus on, what is? How do we discover core metrics for the organizations we support? Imagine that profit or net cash flow happens because you've knocked over a few important dominoes. Those dominoes will be different for every organization based on its mission, vision, and products or services. Yet there will always be a core domino that sits just before revenue. At most for-profit businesses, sales is that core domino. For other types of organizations, the core domino might be patients seen, houses built, loans serviced, resources shared, or students enrolled. These core dominoes are indicators to internal and external stakeholders that the organization is effectively fulfilling its mission.

Core dominoes (core metrics) rarely change, and you must know what they are for your organization. Also, it's helpful to understand (at least at a basic level) the variety of factors that influence the organization's ability to knock over its core dominoes. Employees' actions, behaviors, and performance, as well as how you support these through training and development, will only ever be one factor among many others. Ideally, learning or business leaders will share these factors with the training team. However, leaders may not have clear visibility into what all the factors are. Or perhaps the organization doesn't document factors influencing its core dominoes. In this case, your first step will be to do what I did in the story shared at the beginning of this chapter. Find your core metric. Then make a map showing how the activities done by your learning department may be able to influence your core metric. There is no "right" answer to this exercise. It's simply a way of estimating how activities in your learning department might be supporting the organization's KPIs and core metrics.

If you work for an organization that doesn't document how the organization's KPIs support the business's core metrics, start this project now. Doing this work (even if it's incomplete) and sharing your map with other business units and business leaders demonstrates your commitment to being a strong business partner. Work with others over time to create an accurate depiction of the work.

Change is an unavoidable part of operating a business. However, it shouldn't be an excuse to not measure your contribution to the organization's core metrics. If you have a map in place showing the innerworkings of all your department's activities and how they support the core metrics, then you can easily see how your activities and initiatives might need to change when KPIs change. If your department speaks the language of the business and knows how it uniquely contributes to the core metrics, you can lean into change instead of experiencing it as a setback.

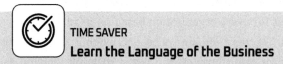

TIME SAVER
Learn the Language of the Business

Every learning professional should be given a scavenger hunt as part of their onboarding experience to learn the language of their business. In his 2023 book, *Aligning Instructional Design With Business Goals*, Kristopher Newbauer suggests finding the answers to these questions:

- Why did the business come into existence?
- What is the business's mission and vision?
- Who does the business exist to serve?
- What needs does the product or service satisfy?
- What are the business's core competencies?
- What are the primary sources of revenue and expenses?
- Whom are the business's biggest customers and greatest competitors?
- How is the business performing now on its KPIs?
- What are the greatest challenges and threats to the business?

Use ROE to Foster Stakeholder Relationships

A program is considered a success if the intended outcomes are achieved. One simple way to evaluate whether your expected outcomes were achieved, while fostering stakeholder relationships, is to use the ROE methodology. It's a great approach for when you're unable to create an impact hypothesis but still want to show the value of your program to stakeholders.

Whose expectations should you prioritize in the ROE methodology, and how do you calculate and report the returns? The answer lies in who is served and supported through your programs. In your role as a learning professional and program manager, whom do you serve? Your immediate answer is likely your learners, participants, or clients. While you serve all those who are involved in the design and development of a learning program, you also serve anyone who may benefit from the program's success. I think of these groups of people as the benefactors of a program's success.

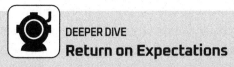

DEEPER DIVE
Return on Expectations

The exact origins of the ROE concept are debatable. Wendy and Jim Kirkpatrick encourage L&D professionals to use ROE and wrote about it in online articles and their 2016 book *Kirkpatrick's Four Levels of Evaluation*. The ROE method is also well documented in Valerie Anderson's 2007 book *The Value of Learning: From Return on Investment to Return on Expectation.* (Note: The ROE methods I write about in this section are my own interpretation and not based on their work.)

The challenge of calculating ROE is that one initiative often has multiple intended outcomes. You might know some of them if they've been shared with you or were revealed in a needs analysis. Other outcomes are unexpressed expectations among those who are invested in your program. It's essential you go into a project with clear expectations on what success looks like from as many interested and invested parties as possible. Doing so increases the probability that your program is designed, delivered, and evaluated in alignment with your benefactors' expectations.

The easiest way to uncover your program's known and unexpressed expectations is to explore the answers to these questions:

- Who may benefit from your program's success?
- What do they need?
- What do they expect will happen during the program and after it's over?

These questions are often included in a needs assessment. However, you may not receive buy-in or the ideal amount of time to conduct a thorough needs assessment. If you find yourself in this situation and want to show the outcomes and value of your program, answering them should be your priority.

Whose expectations are important for you to investigate? There are four groups of people you can easily identify for your initiatives. The first three are:

- **The end user**—your learners or participants
- **The business or community stakeholders**
- **Your learning team**—who want to know their learning experience design is working as intended

Heidi Kirby, a learning evangelist and the founder of Useful Stuff, says there is one more benefactor you shouldn't leave out: **SMEs.** They are often current or former business leaders, valued customers, prospective clients, high-performing employees, researchers, or community members whose personal experience provides rich invaluable expertise. Their input is an incredible asset for learning leaders and program developers to use to shape and inform the content, delivery, and overall experience of programs. SMEs, along with end users and business or community stakeholders, can be great advocates for the adoption and advancement of your programs.

Now that we've identified the four most important benefactors of your programs, you're ready for the next step in the ROE process: identifying needs, expectations, and metrics for data collection and analysis. Each benefactor likely has a different definition of success and unique needs and interests in your program. If you don't start projects by identifying what success looks like and gather critical needs and expectations from the key benefactors' perspectives, you risk wasting time and increasing the overall project costs.

I recently worked with a client to build their membership program—which consisted of digital courses, live group coaching, virtual community meetups, and asynchronous content—in a new technology platform. In the project kickoff meeting, we agreed that it would be successful if we could onboard members in the new tech platform by a specific date (less than four weeks away). Time to onboarding was the critical metric. This made sense from the business stakeholder's perspective. Going into the project, my client knew that current customers had been asking for a virtual member experience for quite some time. So, they wanted to deliver that feature before the end of the calendar year (because that's when many customers decide if they want to renew their membership). The client thought they would retain more members by onboarding them into a new virtual member experience.

What do you notice about the project description? First, in the project kickoff, we prioritized only business needs and expectations. We did not consult end users to think through success from their perspective. We also did not consult SMEs, who helped create the content and craft the member experience, to explore what a successful virtual member experience might look like from their perspective. What do you imagine happened with this project? Well, my client hit their time to onboarding goal and successfully onboarded a group of current customers into the new virtual member platform. However, only 20 percent of end users engaged in the platform after they were onboarded. My client received emails from customers who were confused by the membership platform and what they were supposed to do with it. They did not accomplish their membership retention goals in the new year.

After a failed first attempt, we started all over again. In the second membership project, my client and I took extra time to outline what success would look like from the end-user perspective. We got a diverse group of stakeholders together and brainstormed what the end users needed and what they expected to get out of their membership experience. We then leveraged SMEs and learning design talent to collect insights on what they expected and imagined success would look like. With this information, we decided to pivot away from two different tech platforms and move onto a completely different one. We crafted a high-touch, personalized onboarding experience to ensure all members understood the benefits and tools, as well as how to navigate the platform to make the most of their membership.

By mistakenly prioritizing only the needs and expectations of the business, the project cost four weeks of salaries for everyone working on it. My client also lost trust with a handful of customers and paid two to three times more for technology than was necessary. When you're working on a shoestring and feel pressured by time, have small teams, and maybe lack the ideal expertise, it's easy to cut corners. However, I've found that I always save time and money by investing in a thorough up-front analysis of needs, expectations, and visions of success from multiple perspectives. This process doesn't have to take long. In a thoughtfully facilitated one-hour meeting with representatives from each of your benefactor groups, you can likely obtain all the information you need to proceed with your ROE plan (as well as ideas for purposeful instructional design).

Table 6-1 shows how I applied the ROE methodology to this membership project. It features eight metrics representing the expectations for all the benefactors of the membership program. These were our program's health metrics, and we reviewed them weekly in our program team meetings. For any metrics that we found concerning, my client and I took time to discuss what was contributing to the less-than-ideal performance and what we could do to improve the outcomes. If you are a department of one, or completely new to this process, managing so many metrics for one program or project might seem overwhelming. To simplify it while still getting the benefits of ROE, start your ROE methodology by identifying one metric from each benefactor. As you become more comfortable managing one metric for each benefactor, or have more bandwidth, you can add more metrics. But, remember adding more metrics is only better if they are important to your benefactors.

Table 6-1. ROE Strategy for New Virtual Membership Project

Business Expectations	
Success Definition	Exploratory question: *If the project or program is a wild success, what does that look like?* 1. 80 percent of users are actively using the membership platform every week. 2. Active members are referring new members to the membership platform.
Needs	Exploratory question: *What does the business need from this project or program?* The business needs to increase revenue.
Expectations	Exploratory question: *Once this project or program is over, what do you expect will happen?* Current member retention rates should increase, especially at high turnover times (like end of year and after the first month of membership).
ROE Metrics	1. Percent of current members actively using the membership platform on a weekly basis 2. Number of new member referrals 3. Revenue 4. Member retention rates
Data Storytelling Strategy	Create a bar graph representing the following metrics week over week: 1. Percent of current members logging in to the platform week over week. Are 80 percent or more members logging in? 2. Number of new members who joined via referral. Are there more referrals following the membership program launch? 3. Revenue. Has revenue increased since the membership program launched? 4. Member retention. Are rates of retention increasing or staying the same since the membership program launched?

Table 6-1. (cont.)

Learning Team Expectations	
Success Definition	Exploratory question: *If the project or program is a wild success, what does that look like?* 1. 80 percent of users are engaging in the platform every week. 2. The number of questions or troubleshooting tickets should decrease because customers are getting the information they need from the membership platform.
Needs	Exploratory question: *What does the learning team need from this project or program?* The learning team needs to save time addressing troubleshooting tickets by getting customers to use the membership portal instead.
Expectations	Exploratory question: *Once this project or program is over, what do you expect will happen?* The learning team wants to explore if they can retire their current troubleshooting ticketing system and manage all customer questions on the new membership platform.
ROE Metrics	1. Percent of current members actively using the membership platform on a weekly basis 2. Number of troubleshooting tickets submitted on a weekly basis 3. Number of support questions asked on the membership platform
Data Storytelling Strategy	Create a bar graph representing the following metrics week over week: 1. Create a double bar graph showing the relationship of the number of trouble tickets submitted to the number of support questions asked on the new member platform. Is the number of troubleshooting tickets going down while the number of support questions goes up? 2. Calculate the total percentage of customers logging in to the membership platform each week.
End User Expectations	
Success Definition	Exploratory question: *If the project or program is a wild success, what does that look like?* 1. Ability to meet new members easily 2. Ability to share referrals with other members
Needs	Exploratory question: *What does the end user need from this project or program?* Easier onboarding and ability to find what they need on the platform

Table 6-1. (cont.)

Expectations	Exploratory question: *Once this project or program is over, what do you expect will happen?*
	To have easy access to and timely responses from program mentors and coaches
ROE Metrics	1. Amount of referral business exchanged among members 2. Rate of ease navigating the platform 3. Average length of time coaches take to respond to members on the platform
Data Storytelling Strategy	Create a bar graph showing the following data points week over week: 1. Number of referrals shared on the platform 2. Star rating out of 5 showing how easy it is to find what they need on the platform 3. Number of hours on average it takes coaches to respond to members
SME Expectations	
Success Definition	Exploratory question: *If the project or program is a wild success, what does that look like?*
	Members will receive relevant, high-quality, and original information to support their goals of business growth.
Needs	Exploratory question: *What does the SME need from this project or program?*
	To have input developing the program
Expectations	Exploratory question: *Once this project or program is over, what do you expect will happen?*
	1. 80 percent of members using the platform 2. An increase in member retention
ROE Metrics	1. One piece of original content shared weekly on the platform 2. SMEs invited to all program meetings 3. 80 percent program engagement rate 4. Increase in number of members retained
Data Storytelling Strategy	There's no need to add any metrics to the dashboard demonstrating the program outcomes (ROE). Metrics 1 and 2 are activities that will be systematically incorporated into the membership management process. Metrics 3 and 4 are already being tracked from the business perspective.

Let Good Data Build Stakeholder Partnerships

We must create solutions to pervasive problems by working multiple angles. Build relationships with people you know will be your greatest advocates at the ground level: on the floor, in the field, and on the front line. To nurture relationships from the top down—at the C-suite level—you must let the data advocate on your behalf. But, the data that's easiest to access may not be what C-suite leaders want to see.

Megan Torrance, author of *Data and Analytics for Instructional Designers*, helps us understand the different types of data and analytics needed to tell the learning impact story. We need to tie a few buckets of data together to show L&D's contribution to the business: data on learning, performance, business operations, and strategic results (Table 6-2).

Table 6-2. Types of Data Required to Show Learning's Contribution to the Business

Learning	Performance*	Business Operation	Strategic Results
• Enrollment • Completion • Activities • Learner satisfaction • Test scores • Learning time • Goal achievement	• Procedures and processes followed • Job competencies • Communication • Productivity • Conflict resolution • Inclusivity	• Quality metrics • Cost metrics • Brand metrics • Customer loyalty • Market share • Employee satisfaction • Retention	• Profit • Revenue • Total costs • Reputation

The examples of performance data are umbrella metrics. Each one needs to be defined operationally so it's specific enough to be measured accurately. See Chase's story in chapter 2 for how to create specific metrics from performance outcomes.

Let's revisit the hypothesis framework from chapter 1 for crafting a clear vision of your program's short- and long-term outcomes. That framework includes four similar buckets: program completion, changes in mindset or capabilities, short-term outcomes, and long-term outcomes (Figure 6-1). The data you need to prove your hypothesis can be found in learning, performance, business operations, and strategic results. Even though learning data is the easiest to access (you'll find much of it inside your LMS), business leaders don't care as much about learning activities. They want to see how learning activities influence business activities. It's your job to show them this correlation. Doing so will work wonders in nurturing your relationships with C-suite business leaders.

Figure 6-1. Impact Hypothesis Framework

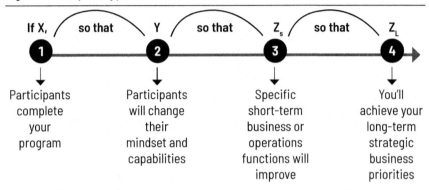

Accessing performance and business data can be tough. Don't worry about the short- and long-term outcome data at first. If you're working as an internal employee, you likely won't have access to this data unless you can give the gatekeeper a compelling reason why. And if you're working as a third-party vendor, getting access to a client's business data is nearly impossible. The goal is not to spend energy getting access to this data, but to collect learning and performance data that allows you to show a strong relationship among those variables. The example in Table 6-3 covers the manager development program referenced in chapter 1. Chase wanted to teach new managers delegation skills to better balance their workloads and ultimately prevent burnout and turnover.

What do you notice about the learning and performance data for the manager development program? Here's what I see:

1. Most new managers completed the program and found it useful.
2. 80 percent built the habit of evaluating their workload every week.
3. Only 50 percent of new managers who worked more than 40 hours a week were able to find a task to delegate.
4. Of the managers who did identify a task to delegate, 100 percent successfully prepared for their delegation conversations.

Table 6-3. Examples of Learning and Performance Data

Learning Data	• 80 percent of participants completed the program. • 95 percent of participants said the program was a worthy investment of their time. • 75 percent of participants believed the learning experience was useful for helping them facilitate delegation conversations.
Performance Data	**Performance Focus 1:** • Activity: New managers will reflect on their workload at the end of every week. Did they work more than 40 hours? What is their stress level? • Output: After four weeks, 80 percent of managers evaluated their workload every week, sharing how many hours they worked and their level of stress.
	Performance Focus 2: • Activity: New managers will identify one task they can delegate when they reach or move beyond their workload capacity (working more than 40 hours each week). • Output: After four weeks, 50 percent of managers who worked more than 40 hours a week identified a task to delegate.
	Performance Focus 3: • Activity: New managers will prepare for a delegation conversation by coordinating all the information and expectations to share with their direct report. • Output: After four weeks, 100 percent of managers who selected a task to delegate were prepared for delegation conversations.

If I were the designer accountable for this program, I would be digging into why new managers struggled to identify delegation opportunities and then update my curriculum to address those problems for future sessions. I can also see that overall the program accomplished its intended performance goals. This means I have 50 percent of the chain of evidence (or data) necessary to show learning impact (learning data and performance data). To get the second half of the necessary data (business operations data and strategic results data), it's time to do one of two things: If you're an internal employee, schedule a conversation with your data gatekeeper. (If you're unsure who can help you access the right operations and strategic results data, invite an operations manager out for coffee and ask them if they might be able to help you get the data you need). If you're a third-party vendor, you need to do some research.

For internal professionals, a conversation with an operations leader (or perhaps even your boss) can get you one step closer to the operations and business data. Here's an example of how that could go:

> "I understand that we have been experiencing a high amount of turnover with new managers because they are feeling burnt out (this was the reason for the delegation training). I have a hypothesis that the delegation skills training might help reduce burnout and turnover. If you look at the data I collected from the most recent program, you'll see that participants who completed it improved their capacity for managing their workload through delegation. I'd like to test the idea that new managers who complete this training stay longer than managers who didn't get this development opportunity. Do you know who can help me access new manager retention data so I can compare it?"

If I were the leader on the receiving end of this question, I would not only be impressed by your initiative to make data-driven decisions, but I would also happily introduce you to whomever could grant access to retention data. Why? Because you provided a compelling reason. And you'd done half of the work already, showing how learning clearly improved performance.

For external L&D professionals, the easiest way to access business data is by using a secondary dataset, rather than your client's data directly. Your goal is to show that improving delegation skills positively influences new manager retention (because retention is the problem your program was designed to solve). This relationship is something researchers in business, academia, and human performance improvement have explored in the past. All you need is a library card, a friend currently enrolled in a higher-education program, or Google Scholar to access this secondary data.

Measuring learning is much easier if you simply remove a core obstacle. Use secondary data instead of trying to access a client's business data. Don't attempt to access business data within your own organization until you've done the work to show that your programs are improving performance in ways that are beneficial to the business. To build stronger relationships with stakeholders at the C-suite level, all you need to do is measure changes in behavior and performance.

Know Your Metrics and Your Targets

It's no secret that business leaders are primarily concerned with ROI. They are constantly making decisions on how to manage revenue and expenses to optimize the business. Thus, asking, "Will this activity offer a good ROI" is an important practice for learning professionals. I've already mentioned that lack of time and resources is one of the top 3 challenges to measuring learning outcomes (especially outcomes reflecting behavior or performance changes and business impact). The investment L&D professionals are often balancing is time, not money. So, to better manage your time, you must go one step beyond creating metrics to also establishing clear targets.

Targets give you permission to shift your focus and support underachieving performance or operations needs. They also empower L&D to make their own decisions about how to allocate their time. If you don't currently have targets, you're probably wondering how to create them. I suggest you schedule a meeting with a manager in your organization's marketing department. Your goal in this conversation is to come up with a process for creating targets for the learning function. Have an informational interview with the marketing manager, and ask them these questions:

1. How did you (or business leaders generally) come up with targets for your KPIs?
2. What are the some things you considered when creating targets?
3. What happens if the department doesn't hit the targets?
4. How often are the targets updated?
5. For the targets that are met regularly, what do you believe contributed to that success?

Humans seem to have a bad habit of trying to reinvent the wheel. The process of creating targets is not unique for L&D. We should leverage the knowledge and experience of others who created targets before us. All departments in an organization (marketing, operations, sales, and IT) have core metrics and targets. Select someone you have a good relationship with in any other department, buy them lunch, and ask them how they created and currently manage targets for their department. Then, once you've created your own targets, share them with the same department leader and ask for their feedback. You don't have to do this work alone!

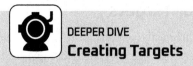

DEEPER DIVE
Creating Targets

If you want more guidance on creating targets with great templates and examples, read *Partner for Performance* by Ingrid Guerra-López and Karen Hicks (2017). In the appendix, you'll find a template from their book demonstrating how to create targets for your next training initiative.

A Shoestring Summary

When you find yourself in situations with limited stakeholder partnership, remember to think like a business unit first and a learning unit second. The learning function is a business unit just like any other department in the organization. Our primary goal as learning professionals is to help the organization be successful by creating optimal working environments and nurturing talent. What is often missing when we lack partnerships with stakeholders is clear visibility into how learning supports the business. While it may not be explicitly written in the learning professional's job description, we can build business acumen and help all benefactors of learning see how our learning activities are supporting the organization's core metrics. The following action steps can help you begin building this visibility for yourself and others:

1. **Show stakeholders you genuinely care about the business.** You should not expect stakeholders at any level (C-suite, learners, SMEs, facilitators, or managers) to do the work for you to connect the learning function to business outcomes. The value of learning is not in the learning itself. Remember, learning is a means to an end, and that end is what all stakeholders care about. You should care about the outcomes of learning just as much as, if not more than, they do. Sometimes, that means walking the floor, shadowing in the field, or meeting C-suite leaders halfway by using data to show how learning contributed to performance changes that meaningfully support strategic business goals.

2. **Find your core metric and create your own targets.** It is OK to prioritize and pivot. Everything you do in the learning function

should be directly in service of (or at a minimum complementary to) a business's core metrics.

3. **Remember, your biggest stakeholders and advocates for the L&D function may not be sitting in the C-suite.** Senior leaders are important stakeholders, yet they aren't the only ones you should care about. Balance trickle-up and top-down approaches to building relationships with stakeholders and partners throughout the business, and the possibilities for your L&D function will surpass your wildest expectations. And don't forget, building and maintaining these relationships takes consistency. Your relationships with stakeholders aren't a means to an end—they are your long-term partners in success.

7
Investing (or Not) in External Expertise

Build it or buy it? All business leaders face this question when they observe gaps in employee skills, operational systems, and technology infrastructure. Learning professionals face this question when they lack the tools, technology, expertise, or people to design, develop, facilitate, and evaluate their programs. There is always a cost associated with building or buying the support, tools, and systems necessary to sustain and scale learning programs. When evaluating learning on a shoestring, the decision about whether to build it or buy it isn't all based on cost. The real consideration is what value you get in the short- and long-term after building it or buying it. The short- and long-term value is your guide to determining whether buying external support is worth the investment.

The L&D industry is susceptible to shiny object syndrome. There will always be a new idea, methodology, tool, or technology claiming to improve learning design, delivery, and outcomes. If we never adapt our L&D strategies using new methods and technology, then our learning outcomes will surely suffer. The question is not whether we should or should not adopt new tools and methods. The real questions are why and when. Don't be swayed by the promised value of new ideological or technological resources. Instead, calculate in advance the short- and long-term value of a resource by using a clear vetting process (Table 7-1). This will help you confirm you have the right reason (why) and that it's the right time (when) to buy external support.

Table 7-1. Build It or Buy It Cost-to-Value Estimating Process

Build It	Buy It
What does it cost?	
Initial build costs include: • Staff salaries • New tools or technology • Systems support and integration	Initial set up costs include: • Onboarding support • One-time initiation fees • Overlapping costs associated with terminating one contract, account, or subscription and migrating to another
Monthly or annual costs include: • Staff salaries for maintenance • Technology subscription fees • Systems support and integration fees	Monthly or annual costs include: • Access to third-party support • Technology subscription fees • Systems support and integration fees
Time considerations: • How much time will you need before you can begin using a minimum viable product (MVP)? • What is your initial cost to value ratio? (total initial costs divided by time to MVP)	Time considerations: • How much time will you need before you can begin using a minimum viable product (MVP)? • What is your initial cost to value ratio? (total initial costs divided by time to MVP)
What is the short-term value?	
• Skill development opportunities for all staff involved in the project • Increased accountability and control over the project deliverables and outcomes • Possible refinement and clean-up of systems and programs involved in the build-it process	• Increased probability of time to value • Less staff time dedicated to the project • Access to expert support
What is the long-term value?	
• Upskilled staff can lead and support future build-it initiatives • Ownership of products and data • Ability to sell or repurpose anything built internally	• Products, programs, and other outcomes can be accomplished on time by leveraging external support • Establishment of a trusting relationship with an external vendor that understands the business and can be called on for future projects

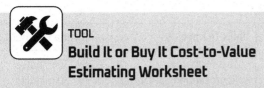

TOOL
Build It or Buy It Cost-to-Value
Estimating Worksheet

In the appendix, you'll find a blank worksheet you can use to map out your own decision-making process.

Once you've outlined the costs and the probable short- and long-term value associated with building or buying support, you're ready for the vetting process to begin.

Solve the Build or Buy Conundrum With Time to Value

While working on a data-enabled curriculum project, I hit a bump in the road. The data visualization tool I originally imagined using would not work. I was faced with a build it or buy it conundrum. Should I teach myself how to use a new data visualization tool and build the learning outcome dashboards myself? Or should I find someone else with more expertise and pay them to build the dashboards instead?

To determine the best path forward, I needed to calculate the time to value (TTV) for my two options. First, I needed to clarify what value looked like. Whether I built the dashboards or bought them, I had to get the same minimum value out of the investment. The following questions guided me in determining the TTV:

- What functions will the completed product (in this case, my data visualization dashboards) ideally provide for you?
- What must you be able to do to make each function possible?
- How much time will it take you to become proficient in each activity?

Table 7-2 uses my data visualization dashboarding project to demonstrate how the TTV equation could work.

Table 7-2. Build It TTV Equation

Dashboard Functionality	Skills to Develop	Time Estimate
Text summaries will show comparisons of outcome variables across two or more time periods.	• Text formatting • Representing data as text • Creating summary sheets to calculate all summative data values	• 30 minutes • 30 minutes • 8 hours
Changes in outcome variables across two or more time periods will be presented graphically.	• Building scatter plots, bar graphs, and pie charts • Visual formatting of graphs	• 2 hours • 30 minutes
The dashboard will be formatted with page numbers, titles, logos, and brand colors.	• Adding logos, page numbers, and titles on all pages	• 30 minutes
The dashboard will include a drop-down menu showing the results of different participant groups.	• Organizing and representing data according to unique groups	• 1 hour
Results can be displayed by learner demographics and personal characteristics.	• Slicing data views by two or more different characteristics	• 2 hours
Learners can receive a personalized link to the dashboard to view their results data.	• Creating links for each individual user to view their own unique data	• 1 hour
Totals		
Total estimated time		16 hours
Buffer for unanticipated time (approximately 10%)		2 hours
Total time invested in building expertise		18 hours
Total cost invested (hours x hourly rate)		$1,800

Once you've completed the estimation work, you should ask yourself a few more important questions:

- Do you have the time necessary to build both the expertise and the product you need to achieve the desired outcomes?

- If you build the expertise and the product yourself, will the product have the minimum viable quality to achieve the desired outcomes?
- Does investing the time to build the expertise and product yourself set you up for success in future projects? Or will the expertise or product only be used for this project or in rare instances?

If you can answer yes to each question, then you can give yourself the green light to build the expertise or product yourself. If you answer no to the first question, then building the expertise isn't a good option unless you can extend the project deliverable deadline. The third question is an important part of the build it or buy it decision: Will you use these skills or products again in the future? If this is a one-off project or unique skill set not likely leveraged in the future, buying the expertise or product is probably a better option.

What did I end up doing with my data visualization conundrum? I calculated the TTV and found that I had a very quick turnaround to build both the expertise and the product. Tight deadlines often produce a high-stress environment in which you're more likely to make mistakes. I didn't want to put myself or my clients in a risky position, so I opted to hire an expert to build the data visualization dashboards. However, I did it with a slight twist—I hired an expert who was willing to teach me and record their work while they were building the dashboards. This didn't require much added time for them and was well worth it for me. Thus, I chose to delegate building the first few dashboards to an external consultant, but in the future, I planned to do all dashboard design and client revisions myself.

I later learned from my clients that the data visualization plan we created was perfectly suited for the first use case. However, it wasn't a sustainable solution because it wasn't applicable to future iterations of their programs. For programs in a constant state of evolution, the dashboarding tool I selected would be too costly to sustain due to the hefty amount of revisions required as programs change. The company needed a more agile solution. Thus, had I invested time learning how to use the new data visualization tool, I wouldn't receive the future benefit of applying my newly developed skill set.

I learned a valuable lesson from this experience. Assume program evaluation plans (just like the programs themselves) will need to be easily revised. Create a data collection and visualization solution that won't cause errors, increase the amount of data cleanup, or make comparing past and future data overly difficult.

So, what did I do to explore more agile data visualization solutions? I paid an expert for an hour of their time to help me select a more appropriate strategy. That hour with the expert saved me countless hours researching tools. Sometimes it's worth investing in expertise just to bypass the frustration that can come with stepping into new territory.

Using the TTV equation to explore short- and long-term value can help you anticipate probable consequences of hiring an expert versus building something yourself. If you do opt to hire external expertise, there are a few best practices that will help you find the right person (or organization) for the job.

Identify Your Gap

Once you've made the choice to hire external support, it's easy to get lost in the weeds taking your first step in the hiring process (especially if you have limited experience working with external vendors). I suggest you start by identifying your gap. Joe Harless (1998) advises starting any program development process by asking, "What do we want to accomplish and what is the gap between our current and desired accomplishments?" You can use the same line of questioning to clarify what an external consultant should accomplish and the current gap between what is and what should be with your project.

Unlike fulltime employees, who are hired based on a desired skill set, you hire consultants for their product outputs. The quality of those product outputs is determined by the quality of product inputs—the information you share to guide a consultant in creating the ideal solution. Talented consultants often use strategic questioning to source necessary information in a project discovery conversation. However, they can only source information you have access to. Before engaging in project discovery conversations with prospective vendors or consultants, answer the first few questions of Harless's front-end analysis with your team (which we covered in chapter 4):

- What is the ultimate purpose and goal of the project?
- What should project stakeholders (the business, end users, and your team) be able to accomplish after the project is complete?
- What is the gap between current accomplishments and desired accomplishments?

- What are the root causes of this gap?
- What solutions or initiatives might be able to solve the root causes?
- How will you know if the root causes have been solved?
  (This will offer indicators to evaluate the external vendor or consultant's work.)

Answering these questions will greatly increase the chance that you hire the right external support and they'll deliver a product that fills the gap between where you are today and where you want to be.

Make the Case to Buy External Expertise

Conducting a front-end analysis helps you make the business case for hiring external help. Business leaders are familiar with the build it or buy it conundrum. They usually have a preference to build or buy solutions based on their leadership philosophy and personal experience. For some leaders, hiring external support has always paid off, so they'll have little resistance to your request. Other business leaders prefer looking internally for solutions to organizational problems. As you might imagine, making the business case for external support among leaders that favor internally sourced solutions will be more difficult.

The results of a front-end analysis—specifically the root causes of the accomplishments gap and ideas for viable solutions—help you show business leaders whether you and your team have the time and expertise to fulfill your desired accomplishments. Use the build or buy it storyboarding exercise we covered in Table 7-1 to create a preliminary TTV and estimated cost calculation to present to your supervisor. This demonstrates you've done the deeper thinking and determined that hiring external support will be a good use of time and money. It's possible that, after presenting the TTV and cost estimates to your supervisor, you get permission to change your current focus and make time to build your own skill set if it's something the organization wants to leverage in the future. (As a bonus, you may also get a promotion and new work opportunities—all because you calculated the probable TTV and cost of hiring external support versus internal development.)

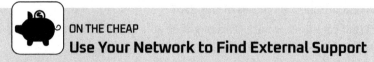

ON THE CHEAP
Use Your Network to Find External Support

Once your budget is approved, you can use your LinkedIn network (or other professional online network) to source support quickly. You likely aren't the only one who has sought that form of support. Post a very clear job description and the outcome you seek (your project accomplishments) in a few L&D groups and to your own followers. You don't need to hire an expensive consulting firm. There are probably many people around the globe who have the skill set you are seeking and would be happy to support you on a freelance or contractual basis. I used this approach for my data visualization dashboards, and I found two amazing consultants whom I still collaborate with.

Testing External Expertise

Many people will say they can help you. Make them prove it! When vetting external sources of support, you should compare fees, production time, and past client testimonials. However, one overlooked part of the vetting process is validating you are getting the right expertise and quality you need for your project to be a success.

Once you have a list of people to interview, invite them to demonstrate their skills and work products. Please note, this suggestion comes with a warning: Working with small businesses, freelancers, and contract workers is often the cheapest and most reliable source of external support—but they are the most vulnerable. As a small business owner and consultant, I am regularly asked to show case studies, project portfolios, and even answer a series of open-ended questions sharing possible solutions as part of the external expert vetting process. This is a standard procedure, with one exception. Sometimes discovery conversations and project demonstrations that appear to be part of a vetting process are just people taking advantage of free expertise. While I encourage anyone (small business owners and corporate leaders alike) to vet external experts, select a reasonable vetting exercise that enables you to get an idea of their work product without asking them to give you something for free.

Now, how can you create the perfect expertise vetting exercise? When I sought an external expert to build data visualization dashboards, I asked myself two questions to learn if the person had the skill set I sought: "Do they have the right expertise" and "Do I like their work quality?"

Because I was hiring an expert to work on one specific technology tool, I asked them to share their screen with me in a virtual interview and show me how they would do three simple tasks with the tool. Before you conduct an interview, I recommend investing a few minutes online to gain a surface-level understanding of the technology tool. This will allow you to see if the consultant has significantly more advanced knowledge of the tool than what you observed online.

I determine quality of work by exploring the strategy someone uses to complete a project and the quality of the visual experience (including whether the project looks visually appealing, is intuitive, is branded appropriately, and makes sense). To do this, ask the prospective consultant to share a recent project they've completed using the visualization tool. Have them walk you through the purpose of the project and why they chose their visualization strategy. I also suggest asking them what challenges they encountered in the project and how they overcame them.

I've mentioned throughout this book that alignment is a key predictor of any program or project's success. External experts often don't have historical or institutional knowledge of your organization, mission, product base, and customers. Thus, you must work intentionally to ensure the products produced by external consultants align with your brand and values, solve the root causes of your problems, and seamlessly integrate with other processes, systems, and programs. Your internal expertise is essential to guide external experts toward creating viable and sustainable solutions. The ideal relationship between internal and external experts is a collaborative partnership in which different voices, perspectives, and skill sets are equally valued. If you think that a prospective external consultant won't be a collaborative partner, move on. When you find someone with the right expertise, work quality, and collaborative mindset, you can make magic together!

Using External Support to Nurture Your Skill Set

One added bonus of hiring external support is the opportunity to leverage their expertise to nurture your own skill set. Of course, not all experts are comfortable or happy being a mentor or taking extra time to teach you. Yet, many will. All you have to do is ask. Job shadowing is the most effective way to learn new skills. With my data visualization project, I specifically hired a consultant who was willing to take me into the "room" with them while they worked. I explained in the original project scope that I was looking for someone willing to spend extra time to teach me how to use the visualization tool. The goals for our work together were to complete two dashboards and to support me in building a working knowledge of the tool. I also included an agreement for the consultant to record themselves while they did specific activities in the dashboard. That way, I could refer to those videos on my own time if I got stuck or to refresh my knowledge in the future.

TIME SAVER
Interview Your External Expertise

Don't assume that all consultants will be open to the "job shadowing" and skill development opportunities. This is a great question to ask as you are interviewing them for the work. If someone isn't willing or comfortable having you shadow them while they work, they are likely not a great fit for you anyway. Consultants who are willing to give back, teach others, and share their knowledge will always be better to work with in the long run.

A Shoestring Summary

We are regularly faced with the question, "Should we build it or buy it?" For professionals working on a shoestring, it can be tempting to assume that building something is cheaper than buying it. I encourage you to always use the cost-to-value estimation worksheet to do some quick math before jumping to conclusions about whether building it or buying it is the better option. You may be surprised which direction you decide to take after spending a few moments thinking through the initial costs, monthly costs, and longer-term value of the build it or buy it investment. Follow the action steps listed here to ensure your investment generates the returns you're looking for:

1. **Calculate the anticipated costs and short- and long-term value before hiring an external expert.** A key theme within this book is that investing a little time up front saves a lot of time in the long run.

For professionals working on a shoestring, investing time up front may seem nearly impossible. Thus, knowing what specifically to focus your energy on helps drive the greatest return on the initial time invested, and it's the same with the build it or buy it conundrum. When you estimate the cost and value of building versus buying, you may learn that building is the better option for long-term value. Conversely, your calculations may help you see exactly how much time building internally might take, as well as whether that time is feasible. Better to find that out before you start building the solution, right?

2. **Identify the gap between where you are today and where you want to be, and the root cause of that gap.** External experts garner their reputation and quality of work by being exceptional in their areas of service. However, even the best experts are not mind readers. Before sourcing external support, use Joe Harless's front-end analysis questions to prepare for your discovery conversations. Providing in-depth knowledge, context, and institutional information leads to a better-quality product.

3. **Build skill development into your project proposals.** Have you heard the saying, "Give someone a fish, and they'll eat for a day. Teach them to fish, and they'll eat for a lifetime"? What if you can get a fish and eat for a lifetime too? Hiring an external consultant who also agrees to mentor and coach you is an ideal combination. By the end of your project, you'll have a high-quality product completed in a timely manner, as well as the skills and resources to complete a similar project on your own in the future.

8

Leveraging Technology and AI to Demonstrate the Value of Learning

Reports from ATD Research, Mind Tools for Business, and Skillsoft have consistently found that technology is a great barrier to measuring learning. Either the technology doesn't report the ideal metrics, the technology stack isn't integrated, or it's not the right technology at all. It's time to stop letting technology hold us back. If the technology that is currently at your fingertips doesn't support your measurement and evaluation needs, then stop using it. Press pause and invest time ensuring you are leveraging the technology you have to its highest and best use: managing administrative work, such as registrations, reminders, time tracking, scheduling, repetitive tasks, data entry, transcription, and meeting notes. The one thing technology can be trusted to do is automate most of your administrative work. Once you've effectively delegated those tasks to technology, you can invest your time to explore and create better systems and processes to measure your program's success.

With the never-ending pace of technology evolution and the accessibility of generative AI, technology will likely always seem like a gift and a frustration. Arielle Kilroy, founder of Dado (an HR technology platform), suggests we focus on what is possible in measurement instead of what is difficult. There's always a way to measure outcomes—don't let technology get in the way of simplicity.

Instead of asking, "What metrics does my technology stack provide?" lean into product thinking and ask, "What are all the possible indicators my program was a success?" With each indicator, you explore what data could be used to demonstrate if you were successful. This data can be found in many places other than your LMS or LXP. For example, an indicator that your new employee onboarding program was successful could be the number of new employees who attend a weekly employee happy hour they learned about during their onboarding. While tracking employee happy hour attendance isn't something technology can do for you (at least not without some prework), it just might be the best metric of success.

Before we dive into more specific best practices for leveraging technology, it is useful to map the types of technologies you could use for different methods of evaluation. Also, some technology tools are more useful (or appropriate) at different phases of your impact hypothesis (which I detailed in chapter 1). The mapping exercise shown in Table 8-1 lays an important foundation to ensure technology helps you save time. In addition, some technology tools won't provide data in each phase of the impact hypothesis. For example, a common misunderstanding is that an LXP or LMS can provide short- and long-term outcome data, but it only offers data on learning activities. You must use other tools or look in other places to find data indicators for growth in KPIs and business goals.

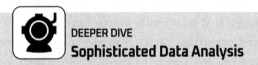

DEEPER DIVE
Sophisticated Data Analysis

The purpose of this book is to offer simple strategies that avoid common challenges caused by complex measurement and evaluation strategies. However, there will be times when you cannot avoid complexity, such as working with big data and managing multiple outcomes. While using an impact hypothesis and clarifying your strategy and tactics will streamline the process of working with big data, you may need more sophisticated hosting, integration, and analysis software than what is outlined in Table 8-1. For help with more complex projects, I recommend reading *Data and Analytics for Instructional Designers* by Megan Torrance.

Table 8-1. Technology Used in Different Phases of the Impact Hypothesis Framework

Phase	Data You'll Seek	Technology Tools
1. Participants engage in the program.	Learning activities and completion rates	• An LMS or LXP
2. Participants advance their KSAs.	Indicators of growth relevant to the KSA you wanted to change	• Survey software • Digital forms • Psychometric assessments • Video evaluation platforms • Automated feedback tools • Chatbots • Spreadsheets
3. The program achieves short-term outcomes.	Indicators of growth in key performance outcomes (e.g., productivity, engagement, and performance activities)	• Business intelligence software • HR platforms • Data hosting software • Data visualization software
4. The program achieves long-term outcomes.	Indicators of growth in business goals or community advancement goals	• Business intelligence software • HR platforms • Data hosting software • Data visualization software

Useful Technology by Evaluation Type

It's helpful to understand the different types of technology tools we might use to create a chain of evidence linking learning activities with short- and long-term outcomes (such as testing the impact hypothesis). Similarly, its useful to explore the variety of tech tools we might use with common forms of evaluation. In the following sections, you'll find a list of common evaluation types. You may use many of them already. For each evaluation type, I've suggested tech tools you can use to collect, analyze, and sometimes even visualize your data (these features will depend on the tech platform you select). As you review these tools, identify which ones you have access to and which ones you don't. In many cases, you can use one platform for multiple types of evaluation. In other cases, you'll save time by using a different tech platform (such as one designed intentionally for a specific type of evaluation).

Self-Reported Evaluations

Self-reported evaluations will generally use a survey, questionnaire, interview, or focus group protocol. What distinguishes this type of evaluation is that you are relying on individual participants to report answers and observations about their own growth and performance.

There are many survey tools on the market. My suggestion is to use the native survey tool for your organization's preferred office software suite (which will usually either be Google Workspace or Microsoft 365). This should work for most of your basic survey needs.

If you need more sophisticated survey tools that feature branching logic, calculations, and formulas, then I suggest getting your entire organization to agree on one tool. The more platforms you use to create surveys, the more data integrations you must deal with, which can quickly get messy.

If you plan to use data from polls in a virtual learning platform, opt instead to create surveys using Typeform, Jotform, or SurveyMonkey. This will allow you to integrate your survey responses directly into Google Sheets. Otherwise, you'll be stuck manually extracting poll data or using an application programming interface (API) integration or Zapier automation to make that poll data useful.

Observation

Observation as a data-gathering tool collects third-party perspectives on participants' growth and performance. Observation is best done using a rubric with clear criteria outlining expectations for excellent and poor performance.

To save time, always use a digital survey to input data from observation rubrics or protocols. This way, you can easily cumulate and analyze the data to calculate individual and group results. The same technology you use for surveys can also be used to create observational rubrics.

Get help creating rubrics for observation using generative AI LLMs like GPT-3.5 of GPT-4. Try the prompt, "Create a rubric used to observe [*insert skill or activity*] on a 5-point performance scale from poor to excellent." You'll need to tweak the response, but it provides a great starting point. The more specific your skill or activity detail, the better your rubric result will be.

Psychometric Assessments

Psychometric assessments are tools you pay for from an assessment vendor. They are valuable because they've often been tested and deemed valid and reliable. Psychometric assessments are available in many subject areas, including soft and hard skills and affective and performance domains.

The trick to using psychometric assessments is understanding the focus area you want to evaluate. A quick online search will reveal to at least one psychometric assessment tool for your topic, whether it's psychological safety, active listening, intercultural competence, problem solving, innovation, creativity, or happiness. Of course, cost will be a consideration in whether you adopt a psychometric assessment. Other things you must consider are whether the vendor is able to prove their assessments are valid and reliable via multiple rounds of testing on diverse sample populations, as well as their ability to integrate results from the assessments to your preferred data hosting solution (for example, Google sheets or your CRM or HRM platform). You do not want to be stuck manually exporting the results of hundreds of assessments into a spreadsheet.

Projects or Case Studies

Project-based learning and case studies are best suited for assessing skills and performance, not knowledge or attitudes. Just like creating clear rubrics when using observation, I also highly recommend creating clear rubrics to evaluate projects and case studies. If the goal is to evaluate skill development, your rubric should have clear criteria to score growth in targeted skills and competencies. Identify what evaluators should look for in the project, which is a clear indicator that growth occurred.

As with observational rubrics, you'll save time in manual data input if everyone doing project-based or case-study evaluations inputs their data into a digital form.

Role Plays

Role plays and simulations are best used to evaluate behavior, performance, and skills. All role-play exercises should have clear rubrics for evaluating behaviors, activities, or performance. Using a digital form to input responses is the best practice for saving time in the data analysis that follows.

Peer Reviews

Peer reviews are a great option for providing feedback at scale, as well as offering alternative perspectives to learners. They're also a good way to evaluate performance and behavior changes. However, I do not recommend using peer reviews alone to evaluate growth in skills and performance. An expert or instructor should also provide evaluative feedback alongside a peer review for optimal reliability.

In addition to the best practices outlined for observation and role plays, one option for peer reviews (if they're done in conversation or audio format) is to record the conversation using a meeting assistant tool like Otter.ai, Zoom, or Microsoft Teams. Then, the conversations can be coded using the program's native AI capabilities to find themes in the feedback, evaluate sentiment, identify keywords, and so on.

The trick to using AI to evaluate conversation transcriptions is to ask good questions. Some examples include, "What sentiment do you observe in this conversation or in this feedback?" and "What themes or keywords are coming up frequently in this conversation?" Then, you can compare the sentiment, themes, and keywords (or any other questions you explore) across all peer review conversations to explore the quality of feedback and whether the feedback aligned with your expectations. You are only limited here by your own creativity.

Simulations

Simulations are a good evaluation tool for high-risk situations. Preparing professionals who work in high-danger roles—such as astronauts, pilots, or operators of heavy machinery—is the best use case for this type of evaluation.

There are many virtual reality and simulation technologies on the market today. If you want to adopt this type of evaluation, ask a technology provider you're vetting to show you case studies that demonstrate the quality level you seek and ensure the data captured from simulations is easy to extract into impact stories and results.

Quizzes or Exams

It is worth noting that quizzes and exams are great for knowledge evaluation but not ideal for evaluating growth in behavior or performance. In addition, knowledge increases are not a predictor of performance growth. Contrary to popular belief, knowledge does not guarantee the accuracy or quality of desired behavior or performance. Practice is the best predictor of the accuracy and performance quality you desire. Hence, role plays and simulations are the greatest evaluation option.

Developing exams is very time consuming. Even with the best technology or the aid of generative AI, you will still invest many hours creating effective exam questions and answer options. If your answer options are poor, then the outcomes of the exam will be a poor reflection of knowledge growth. To save time and increase the validity of your exam, I recommend adopting a valid and reliable assessment from a third-party vendor. However, if you're just using a short quiz for monitoring purposes, developing your assessment in-house may be best.

If you're using a quiz for fun or for monitoring knowledge growth, select a tool that offers an engaging user experience. Many years ago, I used a tool called Kahoot, which featured music, teams, timed questions, and immediately revealed results. The team performance analytics were also great.

The Intriguing Potential of AI

Now that we've established a better understanding of how to use technology tools for unique evaluation and in different phases of the impact hypothesis framework, it's time to dive into generative AI. When asked, "What will be hot in workplace L&D in 2024?" AI was the number 1 response in Donald Taylor's *2024 L&D Global Sentiment Survey.* Interestingly, it was also among the most frequently used keywords when L&D professionals were asked about the challenges facing the industry. There is a lot of hype about using generative AI tools for creating content, preparing training materials, using transcription, and delegating administrative tasks. However, there is less hype (or useful information) about how to use AI to evaluate the outcomes, results, and impact of our programs.

According to McKinsey and Company research on the economic potential of generative AI, it has the capability to replace 60 to 70 percent of the tasks currently done in the everyday working world (Chui et al. 2023). Of course, this estimation is relative to the industry and job, and it is only a prediction. While researchers cannot predict the full potential of AI today, they can anticipate that It will change the experience of work and the global marketplace. After all, in 2023, ChatGPT set a historical record as the fastest growing consumer application.

An August 2023 NovoEd study reported that learning leaders are already using generative AI to delegate some of their everyday activities and four out of five L&D pros want to learn more about using AI in their profession. Here's how learning professionals said they were using AI:

- 38 percent use AI to provide feedback to participants.
- 37 percent create new written training content using AI.
- 30 percent use AI in new-hire orientation.
- 29 percent train workers how to use generative AI on the job.
- 28 percent have developed full courses entirely with generative AI.
- 27 percent produce translations of training content using AI.
- 21 percent create new AI-generated videos.

With the unquestionable power and potential of generative AI (and the many other technologies that are possible because of it), we should regularly ask ourselves how new technologies can improve our work. We also need to think through the consequences (positive and negative) of using these technologies over other solutions.

In truth, we've been asking these questions about new technology for many years now. However, the pace of adoption has rapidly increased, making this new wave of technology feel different than earlier ones. In the past, many L&D professionals excitedly adopted new LMSs and intranets, while others integrated social media into learning experiences. In the early 1990s, the first web-based email platform (Hotmail) became accessible, which caused to email adoption rise. Then, in the early 2000s, mobile phones with email capabilities came to market into the fabric of our everyday lives (Steinbrinck 2023).

What do these waves of technology have in common? Each one was met with an initial level of resistance, followed by mass adoption, and ultimately leading to near full integration within industry sectors in government, education, nonprofits, and corporations alike. This pattern is captured in Everett Rogers's Diffusion of Innovation theory, now popularly known as the Five Stages of Technology Adoption.

Rogers (2003) argues that technology is more readily adopted if it is perceived, or strategically positioned, to be positive and is also similar to recent technologies. His theory helps explain the record-breaking adoption of ChatGPT, for example. It also helps explain why the L&D industry has a bad reputation of quickly pursuing shiny new tools and technology—especially if they are positioned as solving major pain points like engagement, response rates, personalization, and automation. Technology has and will continue to revolutionize many aspects of work and everyday life. As you continue to operate in a data- and technology-rich environment, it is important to adopt a critically optimistic approach to new technology. Doing so will save you time, improve your reputation, boost the quality of your work, and preserve your capacity for critical thinking.

Leveraging Technology With Cautious Optimism

Going back to Rogers's Diffusion of Innovations Theory, I fall in in the early to mid-stages of technology adopters who are cautiously optimistic. When considering a new technology, I'm quick to recognize its challenges and how it can offer solutions, but I like to sit back and wait for the innovators and early adopters to play around with it first. This way I can learn from their insights and be more strategic with when and how I incorporate the new technology into my own work. This also describes the exact approach I've taken with ChatGPT.

In January 2023, a colleague, who is a true technology innovator with a rich Web3 background, excitedly asked me if I'd started playing with ChatGPT yet. He said, "Being an educator and researcher, you must see the many ways in which this tool and generative AI can be useful for your industry." I had yet to fully understand what generative AI was, so I replied, "I'll have to look more into that." Today, I'm still investigating the possible applications of generative AI. Yet this exploration feels different than previous technology waves. For the first time, I'm looking at utility and ethics simultaneously.

The way this exploration unfolded looks something like this. I wondered if ChatGPT could offer an accurate plan for measuring soft skills, so I wrote the following prompt into ChatGPT:

"How would you measure growth in communication skills?"

ChatGPT gave me a lot of great options for evaluating growth in communication skills, including self-assessments, feedback from others, psychometric assessments, portfolio reviews, performance metrics, observations, role plays, and simulations. This was a detailed response. However, the information provided didn't suggest how to collect data for each of the evaluation options.

So, I thought, let's test ChatGPT's ability to recommend how to collect data for one of the suggested options. I gave it the following prompt:

"I would like to use a psychometric assessment. What assessments are available to evaluate active listening?"

ChatGPT offered a list of seven different psychometric assessments that evaluate active listening with a brief description. I discovered that for ChatGPT to offer useful information, I need to state exactly what communication skill I wanted to evaluate and what specific type of evaluation method I wanted to use. Thus, I wrote the following prompt into ChatGPT:

"Write a rubric I can use to evaluate active listening skills in a role-play activity."

In less than five seconds ChatGPT offered a rubric with six different criteria, rated from excellent to poor, including brief descriptions of what excellent to poor looked like for each criterion. The rubric also included a note that said, "This rubric is just an example. Please customize it as needed for your own purposes."

That was impressive! In less than five seconds, I received a work product that might have taken me at least an hour to create myself, and that is with a mastery-level knowledge of active listening. Even more impressive, the six criteria were consistent with much of the best practices about active listening skills and characteristics written in academic journals and other respected publications.

At that point in my experimentation with ChatGPT, I started thinking about the opportunities, implications, and long-term consequences of generative AI tools. This was when utility began intersecting with ethics. I started wondering if I too could be replaced by AI. It works faster and perhaps even more accurately than I can. I closed my laptop and went for a walk, as I often do when I needed to think.

So, what should you be doing to balance the infinite possibilities of generative AI tools with the equally infinite ethical implications of using them? ChatGPT is just one among many technology solutions that can take the time consuming and error-prone tasks associated with measurement and evaluation off your plate. Yet, the most difficult component of measuring program outcomes is something technology may never be able to master (at least not today)—strategic critical thinking. In fact, the presence of new technology, including generative AI, requires a sharpening of our critical thinking skills now more than ever. Let's dive into the core concepts that can help us leverage time- and error-reducing technology while consciously considering the short- and long-term consequences of technology adoption.

Understanding What Makes Generative AI Possible

We live in a world of big data. There are more data artifacts around you than you may be consciously aware of. Your smart watch, smart ring, and fitness tracker all capture your data, oftentimes by the minute, whether about your heart rate, sleep patterns, number of phone calls made, location, music or podcast preferences, and many other data points. Your cell phone tracks even more data. Your credit and debit card purchases are used to capture online spending habits. Activities on social media, streaming entertainment and videogame playing patterns, search history, chat conversations, meetings on your calendar, and email messages—every digital platform captures data on your activities.

I once worked for one of the largest real estate brokerages in the United States, Keller Williams Realty International (KWRI). From its very first day in operation in the early 1980s, all data on agent activities (including listings, sales, and commissions) was hosted and managed in one system. As the brokerage grew and opened franchise offices, it preserved the same rule about all data being hosted and managed within one system. KWRI is now the largest broker-age firm by sales volume and agent count and it has access to more than 40 years of data from agent activities all over the world with which it can make incredible predictions and informed operational decisions, as well as maintain strategic market share. Access to mass amounts of original data made KWRI's success possible. More importantly, its ability to systematically manage that data and use it to make key business decisions enabled its success. Other businesses have made similar operational decisions and are seeing great benefits. For example, Berkshire Hathaway owns and strategically manages its own financial data. It also owns an in-house version of ChatGPT that can analyze data to produce key business insights.

As we discussed in chapter 5, LLMs use a form of generative AI. Models learn from unstructured datasets freely available on the internet (or unstructured data owned and managed within an organization, as in the KWRI and Berkshire Hathaway examples) to make meaning of the world (IBM 2023). The better quality the data, the better quality the insights.

If organizations like KWRI and Berkshire Hathaway represent the highly sophisticated side of data-driven activities, most L&D departments and organizations represent the immature side of data-driven activities. Results from a 2019 learning impact study by Red Thread Research found that organizations with mature learning departments (those that consistently evaluate learning and can demonstrate their impact on the business) are all highly data driven (Mehrotra 2019). Organizations with a mature, data-driven learning function were consistently doing the following activities:

- Identifying appropriate outcome metrics
- Choosing the best sources of data to monitor outcome metrics
- Leveraging all methods available to measure, track, and show impact
- Considering leading and lagging indicators
- Tying learning to business results
- Using data to tell stories of outcomes and impact
- Continuously analyzing and adjusting

To truly reap the benefits of AI and technology tools, we must familiarize ourselves with our data and keep it organized in a meaningful way. I imagine a world in the not-so-distant future in which all organizations have a ChatGPT-like function (akin to Berkshire Hathaway) that sits on top of a large dataset to help them make data-driven decisions. Wouldn't it be great if you could just put a prompt into a generative AI tool and ask things like, "What percent of participants who completed cohort 12 of the sales leader training program increased their sales quota?" or "What do you observe among participants who completed cohort 12 of the sales leader training program that did not increase their sales quota?" I can imagine the tool reporting back things like, "Participants who did not increase their sales quota have not met with their manager since completing the training and have not logged the same number of sales calls as people who saw an increase in sales."

The data to make this type of questioning possible exists today. We can track who meets with their manager and when, the number of outgoing and incoming sales calls compared to the number of sales closed per employee, and the activities employees are doing leading up to closing a sale. Organizations that engage in less mature data-driven activities are simply not strategically or systematically set up to process and use this data in a meaningful way.

If good data increases the usability and viability of technology solutions to help us measure and evaluate our learning programs, then we must increase our access and improve the quality of our data. Follow these steps:

1. Document the data you have and where it's located for each of your programs following the impact hypothesis framework (like the example in Table 8-1). For instance, phase 1 data you have for a new employee onboarding program might look like:
   - In-person meeting attendance can be tracked with an attendance sheet that's manually managed by the HR director.
   - Virtual meeting attendance can be tracked with Zoom.
   - Views of policy documents can be tracked with Microsoft SharePoint.
   - Participant satisfaction scores can tracked with Typeform.

2. Identify what data is currently being managed manually, and translate the data collection method into a digital format. Here are a couple examples:
   - If your HR director uses a pen and paper to have employees sign into in-person meetings, translate this to a Google Form, Microsoft Form, Typeform, or other survey tool that allows people to scan a QR code and place a check mark by their name.
   - If you have students write handwritten thank-you notes to donors, scan the notes into a PDF that can be transcribed into text and populated into a spreadsheet. Use that text to search for themes within students' stories and report cumulative qualitative program outcomes to donors.

3. Once all your data lives in a digital format, find a way to integrate it into one master program or source. Examples of master data sources include:
   - LRSs
   - Spreadsheets
   - HRM platforms

- Salesforce, HubSpot, or another CRM platform that hosts data on your employees, customers, and marketing prospects
- Data hosting and reporting tools like Qualtrics, Tableau, Google Looker Studio, or Microsoft Power BI

4. Test your ability to analyze and query your newly integrated data sources to find insights, patterns, and outcomes among key variables. Try answering these questions:
   - Can you pull reports that show relationships among participants, employees, or customers who completed your programs and KPIs?
   - Can you calculate the percentage of participants, employees, or customers who completed or purchased one of your learning programs?
   - Can you compare the differences in employee engagement among employees who have been retained longer than five years compared with those who resigned in less than two years?

5. After testing your integrated data to find insights, patterns, and outcomes, determine what is getting in the way of making meaning out of your data. Consider these examples:
   - If the data format made it difficult to explore, you likely need to clean it up.
   - If you can't confidently pull reports and query the data, you likely need to invest some time with a coach or consultant to learn how to use the tool you selected to host your data in one location.
   - You might need to invest in both data cleanup and a coach or consultant to get the insights you need from your data source.

Among the major pain points for learning professionals is the lack of integrated data. Your data is likely scattered across numerous platforms, stored in print format, and living in your head after observing participants during and following a training program or having anecdotal conversations. To ready yourself to leverage generative AI and other tech tools, you need to think critically about all the sources of data you currently have access to or could have access to after making a few systematic tweaks. Then, clean up this data by bringing it into a digital format and making everything communicate via integration. Once you've done this crucial step, you'll be able to more easily use the data to show immediate-, short-, and long-term learning outcomes of training programs.

Using AI Where It's Been Tried and Tested

Many studies describing how AI has been used in education (teaching and evaluation) came about in 2020. While those studies are the first of many more to come, they are useful indicators of what's possible. More importantly, the areas where AI use and consequential outcomes are being explored in academic research offer a safer entry point for your own use of AI.

While ChatGPT made generative AI top of mind for the masses, earlier generations of AI have already been used in educational evaluation and assessment. If you're like me and find yourself somewhere between an early and majority technology adopter mindset, you'll find comfort testing AI capabilities and corresponding consequences in four ways: performance support, personalized feedback, automated scoring, and formative assessment.

Performance Support

When was the last time you needed customer support from a large corporation like Delta, Airbnb, or Hotels.com? Yes, those are the last three corporations I contacted online for support. You might have used a chatbot to ask questions and find support articles, or you may have had a full conversation with the chatbot to get your issue resolved. These are great examples of AI performance support.

This technology has been around for a long time and is a wonderful way to save staff time and resources to support employees, students, or community members by connecting them with resources at their time of need. Why does this matter? JD Dillon, author of the *The Modern Learning Ecosystem*, suggests that rather than investing in expensive formal, structured training programs as our go-to recourse, we should first invest in a modern learning ecosystem. The foundational layers of a modern learning ecosystem are a shared knowledge system and performance support. Both layers can and should be facilitated through automated technology and AI (because that's the most cost-efficient way to do it). And what does all this have to do with measurement and evaluation? A shared knowledge system and performance support facilitated by technology can give you data on how people are using these systems. That data can then be integrated into the overall dataset, which tells you how learning opportunities are influencing job performance and business or community outcomes. Investing in a shared knowledge system and performance support saves you time on instructional design so you can allocate your valuable resources to measuring learning outcomes.

TIME SAVER
Getting Ready to Build Your Own Performance Support Tool

Chatbots are the most common performance support tools (as well as the most cost effective to implement). This is a technology you can purchase off-the-shelf from a vendor, rather than develop in-house. However, before you can use a chatbot, you must have good data to train it. If you don't have a place for employees or members of a specific team to ask questions and get immediate feedback, that should be the first performance support tool you invest in. Before buying chat technology, build a manual system to capture all the questions and concerns people have. This could be as simple as creating an email address employees write to with questions. It could also be a designated Slack channel or LinkedIn group to ask questions. Institute this manually managed performance support tool for three to six months or until you have a decent number of questions (and answers) to train your chatbot. This way you'll have confidence that your chatbot has the knowledge to answer most questions it will encounter. Any questions the chatbot can't answer will get sent to a support person, and the AI will receive training too.

Automated Scoring and Formative Assessments

Automated scoring and formative assessments are the low-hanging fruit of AI-based technology tools. When you create your own surveys, quizzes, and even rubrics in most digital survey tools, you get the advantage of using built-in automatic scoring. This means that you can tell survey tools the right answer to your questions and then the tool will automatically grade all surveys and summarize the results.

Formative assessments are quick questionaries that help you understand the skills, personality, or sentiment participants experience in the moment. I personally know at least five people who have created formative assessment tools on a variety of topics. A little online searching will lead you to an automated or AI-based formative assessment for your specific topic. I'd like to warn you, however, that these tools are often low cost or even free for a reason.

Off-the-shelf formative assessments evaluate changes in sentiment and knowledge. These low-level evaluation options leave you with low-value data. To obtain high-level evaluation and high-value data, you need assessment tools that can help you understand changes in behavior, such as simulations, scenarios, role plays, observations, and psychometric assessments.

The best assessments, especially in an era where AI can ace nearly every available standardized test, are methods leading participants to use higher-order thinking skills like analysis, synthesis, creativity, innovation, problem solving, and critical thinking. These higher-order competencies (in contrast to lower-order skills of memorization and recall) are the same capabilities that lead to a more agile and resilient workforce—which is what we need to constantly adapt. Thus, we'll not only encourage deep learning through higher-order assessments, but we are combating one of the current concerns about the influence of AI on educational assessment.

One often overlooked and valuable byproduct of evaluation work is the reinforcement of learning alongside data collection by showing progress toward desired growth and change goals. Assessments can be simple tools that tell educators and stakeholders whether participants increased knowledge, improved skills, or changed their performance after training. They can also be an experience that helps participants refine their skills, challenge their thinking, and solidify new information.

In Julie Dirksen's latest book, *Talk to the Elephant*, she states that a thoughtless or poorly designed assessment tool can undermine an entire learning experience. And she's right! If you complete an assessment (such as an exam, simulation, role play, or coaching conversation) that doesn't reflect the key messages and application goals of the program, and also seems like an afterthought, you're more likely to disregard the significance and value of the program itself.

Many experienced researchers will warn novice professionals that the quality of their research questions will determine the quality of their responses. Dirksen also warns that a low-quality assessment can demean a learning experience. They can also dampen the quality of your data. Thus, whether we write our own assessments or if we use AI, we must practice crafting thoughtful, relevant inputs.

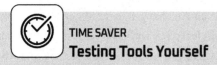

TIME SAVER
Testing Tools Yourself

If you are new to AI and want to use it to automatically score an assessment and give relevant feedback, test it yourself. For example, when I tested a video-assessment tool that used AI to score participants' elevator pitches and give them personal feedback, I quickly learned that I was not inputting detailed enough parameters for the tool to give good feedback. Sometimes, it's easy to forget to or forgo testing your assessment tools yourself. You might be surprised by what you find!

Personalized Feedback

Lack of manager support after formal learning experiences are over is consistently cited as a significant limitation in facilitating the application of new information and skills on the job. This support is a critical piece of the learning predictability puzzle. If managers or tenured peers can support and reinforce the accurate application of new practices, policies, and skills, learning transfer and recall increases. Yet, managers and tenured peers often lack the bandwidth to reinforce training. What if generative AI can fill this gap?

Earlier generations of AI have been used to facilitate feedback. Teachers have reported the ability to provide personalization at scale as a benefit (González-Calatayud et al. 2021). Moreover, this feedback becomes an additional data artifact that can help you evaluate growth and change in participants as they engage in learning opportunities. That data becomes a valuable part of your chain of evidence, tying learning activities to short- and long-term business or community outcomes—if you set up the right systems to integrate assessment and feedback results with other learning and organizational data.

The performance of machine learning and AI is only as good as the data it has to learn from. To offer authentic, valuable feedback in learning, we must train any AI tool by giving it thoughtful, accurate information on what feedback to provide, at what specific time, and under what circumstances. We need to supply mastery-level information to help the AI tool provide mastery-level feedback.

While you can find available AI tools for personalized feedback, I suggest vetting any potential AI tech provider by getting answers to these questions:

- **How is the AI tool trained to provide accurate and relevant feedback? Will the provider supply the data or will you?**
  - In some instances, AI assessment and feedback tools will be subject specific (such as active listening, inclusion, intercultural competence, language learning, or an identified leadership characteristic). Thus, the technology provider might use its own dataset to train and upskill its AI tool. You could ask how many people have taken the assessment, how diverse the sample is, and how it's minimizing bias in the dataset. For example, if an AI tool is trained with biased data, then it will also use that biased perspective when providing feedback. Not unlike a person. The difference is that you can provide professional development to people to help them understand unconscious biases and nurture broader perspectives. The only way you can train an AI tool to be less biased is by ensuring the data it's trained on is broad, diverse, and unbiased.
  - In other instances, you will need to train the AI tool using your own data or inputs. If you are in this situation, you would ask what support the technology provider's team provides to help you input the best information and parameters to reduce time figuring those details out on your own.
- **Will they give you a demo to test out the tool from both the learner and administrator perspective?** Some technology is simply not designed in an intuitive, user-friendly way. If you don't feel comfortable and you can't imagine your learners feeling comfortable using the technology, then it's useless.
- **How do they approach data ownership and privacy?** Many technology companies like to have access to client data so they can make predictions, share insights, and market their products. Are you comfortable with that? Do you get to say how your data is being used? What standards do they adhere to regarding data privacy and security? Remember, data is the new currency. You want yours protected, and in some countries, this is a legal requirement.
- **How can you integrate the assessment and feedback data with other data your business uses to track KPIs?** If they say that you

can download your data into a spreadsheet and upload it to another database, I suggest looking for another provider. You should have a way to use an API to automatically integrate your data. If you must manually manage large amounts of data regularly, it may lead to errors and is unnecessarily tedious.

Just Get Started!

How do you start using AI to enhance measurement and evaluation? First, you should educate yourself on AI's current capabilities. Today, AI can perform the following activities as well as or better than its human counterpart:

- Classify
- Edit
- Summarize
- Answer questions
- Create new content

Select which activities on this list AI could perform on your behalf to reduce time, errors, or cost. Then, keeping these specific activities in mind, look for an AI tool that performs the tasks you need for measurement and evaluation. The good news is that Microsoft and Google have both made major advancements and investments in AI within their product suite. You may just need to do a quick online search to see if Google or Microsoft has the AI capabilities you're looking for and if you can access that AI technology.

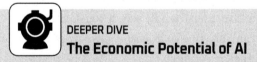

DEEPER DIVE
The Economic Potential of AI

For a fascinating look at AI capabilities and predictions for the future, read McKinsey and Company's June 2023 report, *The Economic Potential of Generative AI.*

There is one important thing I must emphasize before we can reap the value in time and cost savings: You must know what activities you need to execute your measurement and evaluation plans. Some activities can easily be done for you by automation and AI tools, but other activities are best managed yourself. Here are a few immediate opportunities for using AI to maximize the value of your investment:

- Create a shared database of relevant documents that is easily searchable (AI can do the searching).
- Adopt an AI chatbot and train it on the documented policies, procedures, and best practices inside your shared database. For example, you can use videos, meeting transcripts, written documents, and interviews. This becomes an MVP support tool that can be perfected over time as more people use it.
- Explore the administrative activities you are currently doing that can be supplemented by automation or AI tools.
- Use AI to support data analysis. AI can currently synthesize and analyze information in video, text, tables, numbers, and image formats. Theoretically, if all your data is in one location, you could ask an AI chatbot your research questions and get the answers you seek.

Consider these as fundamental first steps to using AI to improve learning experiences and create useful data artifacts to integrate into your measurement strategy. Using automation and AI comes with a great upside, but there are also consequences from leveraging tools with this level of sophistication. As I mentioned at the start of this chapter, technology has now advanced to the point where we are both eagerly experimenting with its utility while pondering the long-term ethical implications for the human race.

TIME SAVER

Generative AI Prompts

Follow current best practices for prompting generative AI tools. To increase the likelihood of a relevant output from ChatGPT (or a similar tool), experts suggest adding these details in your prompt: instruction, context, and output indicator (González-Calatayud et al. 2021).

For example, what was the most popular electric sedan in Australia in 2020?
- **Instruction:** "What is"
- **Context:** "most popular electric sedan"
- **Output indicator:** Australia and 2020 (These are the parameters limiting AI's possible outputs for the context of most popular electric sedan.)

A Shoestring Summary

We live in an exciting time. Data and technology are more accessible and less costly than ever before. While there are many sophisticated, expensive technology tools out there for enterprise-level organizations, there are equally as many tools available for the scrappy L&D professional. Being on a low budget is no longer as great of a barrier to accessing useful technology. The opportunity for those of us working on a shoestring is to keep data collection and technology tools simple from the start. Complexity leads to feeling overwhelmed and more work. Start with a clear strategy for using technology to evaluate your programs and follow the action steps listed here to prioritize your time and energy:

1. **Investigate the data your organization currently uses to track its KPIs.** Find out what the core KPI metrics are for your organization, what data artifacts are used to track progress, and where this data lives. This information is critical to help integrate your learning data with other organizational data. Remember that the future is already here, but most people aren't fully experiencing it yet. You could be just a few steps away from mature data ownership and management strategies, like those at KWRI and Berkshire Hathaway. Taking the initiative to understand how your organization currently manages its data will make it much easier to make informed decisions on what technology to adopt and how to integrate learning data with other KPI data.

2. **Investigate the data your learning department currently uses to track learning activities.** Because you know that most learning departments mainly track data like completion rates, attendance, and satisfaction, start by looking at your LMS or LXP. Or, the data might live in a paper format or a digital format on a shared drive somewhere. Remember the story I shared in chapter 7 about managers who were uploading performance reports? One staff member was drowning trying to keep up with manually inputting performance data into a spreadsheet. Some of this might also be happening in your organization. Find all the data artifacts that could be useful to create a chain of evidence tying program completion to immediate-, short-, and long-term organizational goals. You'll likely be surprised by what you find.

3. **Integrate your data.** Your data is useless unless you can tie it together to tell stories of success, effectiveness, outcomes, and impact. Integrating your data into one place to easily pull reports, create pivot tables, or create dashboards is what makes data storytelling possible.

4. **Prioritize good data over vanity data.** While it's easy to pull superficial metrics and use them to tell a story of outcomes and impact, they can't tell a compelling story of outcomes and impact. Instead, they tell a story of activities—not why those activities matter. Understand the goals and purpose of your program and use those objectives to prioritize collecting data that is essential and can tell you if the programs have accomplished their goals and purpose.

5. **Practice using AI.** There are many ways to integrate automation and AI into your program evaluations. Just start somewhere. Ideally, start with a tool that you think is both exciting and intuitive to use. Once you start with one tool, you'll gain confidence playing around with the utility and consequences (good and bad) of others.

Bringing It
All Together

In a book written for professionals working on a shoestring to make measurement easier, you may be expecting a magic formula to take the pain and frustration out of program evaluation. It is my sincere hope that the impact hypothesis framework I outlined in chapter 1 will serve that function. If you're still hoping I'll tell you about a metric you can apply to all your programs to show the outcomes, impact, and value of your work, I'm going to disappoint you. In truth, the metrics you select, the measurement prescriptions you employ, and the tools and systems you use will all be determined by one thing: the program's goal. This is why I love the impact hypothesis framework, as it guides you to clearly outline what you're doing and why. With your impact hypothesis in place, you can easily select appropriate metrics and data artifacts to determine if the program accomplished its goals.

While there will never be one metric that can (or should) be incorporated into every program evaluation, I can say with confidence there is one process you should always employ before the design, delivery, and evaluation of any initiative. Map the strategy of what you are doing and why. There are many ways to do this, including the impact hypothesis framework. You could conduct a needs analysis. Follow Kevin M. Yates's L&D Detective Kit. Leverage a logic model. Follow the appreciative inquiry method. Implement a project discovery session. Try all of these methods to discover which ones you prefer. You may even create your own process for mapping the strategy of what you are doing and why. Regardless of the process you follow, lead with strategy, not with tactics.

If you start measurement and evaluation plans with the question, "What metrics should I select to evaluate my initiative?" you are leading with tactics—not strategy. If you ask the question, "What metrics should I focus on?" you can easily be swayed by metrics others are using, or what is presently being discussed as the hot new metric on social media. Your metrics are determined by your program goals—not the other way around.

In June 2023, for the first time in the history of educational evaluation, the International Organization for Standardization (ISO) came out with suggested standards for learning metrics. These metrics were based on the Talent Development Reporting principles (TDRp) framework written about in the book *Measurement Demystified* by David Vance and Peggy Parskey. They outline possible metrics for three overarching categories of program goals: efficiency, effectiveness, and outcomes. In addition, the principles cover how to translate your metrics into visual stories of impact using common reporting formats such as dashboards, scorecards, and program evaluation reports.

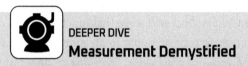

DEEPER DIVE
Measurement Demystified

If you don't own a copy of *Measurement Demystified,* or its companion *Measurement Demystified Field Guide,* you should. They feature many templates and insights about measuring learning outcomes. They're ideal for any professional with intermediate to advanced expertise in measurement and evaluation.

As a professional working on a shoestring, you may sometimes feel like a deer in the headlights—frozen and uncertain about which direction to go—when collecting and sharing evaluation data in a meaningful way. Measurement models and standards are a useful resource to help you select the best path forward. If you're struggling to get started, to try something new, or to make meaning out of large datasets, begin by answering the following questions (even if they may seem counterintuitive):

1. What decision do you want to make?
2. How will you use data to help you make that decision?

One limitation I see with following measurement models is they lead you to believe you're done with your evaluation work once you've analyzed and shared the data demonstrating your program's effectiveness. You surely need to know if your work accomplished its intended outcomes and goals. However, don't stop there! In fact, stopping there diminishes the value of all the work you did to collect data in the first place. In the introduction to this book, I shared two key reasons for investing in measurement and evaluation. First, we need to know if we accomplished our goals. Second, and more importantly, we need to be able to improve the quality and value of our work. This requires us to take one more step after we evaluate the effectiveness of our programs.

Once you know how successful your program or initiative was, what will you do? If you were successful, I hope you'll take a moment to celebrate and add a gold star to your project portfolio. If you weren't, I hope the data helps you understand why. But then what? This is when we turn to the first counterintuitive question. What decision do you want to make? If your program was successful, will you decide to release it to all employees? If your program wasn't successful, will you trash it, revise it, or transform it into something else altogether? How will you use the data you've collected in your evaluation plan to help you make those key decisions? With clarity on the decisions you plan to make after learning whether your program was successful and a high-level strategy of what your program is intended to do and why, you're finally ready to take advantage of the ISO standards and other measurement models.

There is no magic metric to use when measuring and evaluating the outcomes of your programs. However, there is a process you should employ at the start of every project. Lead with strategy—not tactics:

1. Select one of these processes to outline what your program is intended to do and why:
   - Impact hypothesis
   - Needs analysis
   - Kevin M. Yates's L&D Detective Kit
   - Appreciate inquiry method
   - Logic model
   - Front-end analysis
   - Project discovery plan
2. After mapping out what you are doing and why, answer the following questions:
   - What decisions do you plan to make after learning whether your program was successful?
   - What data artifacts do you need to help you make those decisions?

3. With clarity on what you are doing and why, and what decisions you hope to make, consult the ISO learning metric standards to get ideas on what metrics might be most appropriate for your program strategy and post-program decision-making process.

4. Take the Find Your Measurement Match quiz (measurementmadeeasy .com) to help you select the most appropriate measurement model or framework for translating your strategy into the best tactics to calculate the outcomes, impact, and opportunities to improve your programs.

Access the Find Your Measurement Match Quiz at measurementmadeeasy.com or by using this QR code.

Did this book surprise you? Were you expecting to find tools, technology, and time-saving methodologies to make measurement easier? Well, I hope you found some nuggets sprinkled throughout your reading experience. What you likely did not expect was the idea that to build, borrow, and buy support for conducting measurement and evaluation on a shoestring is not solely about cost-saving tools and time-saving technology. Although those resources are useful, making measurement easier comes down to two things: data literacy and critical thinking. We tend to overcomplicate things, and measurement and evaluation is no exception. As a professional working on a shoestring, you must find the smallest, simplest ways to start measuring. If you don't start, don't push yourself beyond vanity metrics, and don't work to incrementally improve your ability to use data to make important decisions, you will not be prepared for the future of work. Worse yet, you won't be able to adequately prepare your employees, students, and members of your community for the future of life and work—because the future (at least from the vantage point we see now) means living in a world in which data is a currency almost as powerful as, if not more than, money.

The process of measurement and evaluation on a shoestring is about prioritizing the most important actions relative to your goals and outcomes. Nothing more, nothing less. You can't do it all. However, you can do what needs to be done. By building your critical thinking, borrowing simple measurement prescriptions when you get in the weeds, and buying support as needed from a marketplace filled with resources—you can build your measurement and evaluation muscles!

The world is ever changing, and it often seems impossible to keep up. Yet, keep up, assess, predict, and make agile decisions we must!

APPENDIX
TOOLS AND TEMPLATES

Use the following templates to help conduct your next project:

- Impact Hypothesis Framework
- Questions to Identify Your Hypothesis Variables
- Learning Strategy Tracker
- Measurement Map
- Question Criteria Checklist
- Self-Reported Evaluation Behavior Change Evaluation Plan
- Data Triangulation Exercise
- Data Triangulation Strategy Checklists
- Results and Gaps Template
- Build It or Buy It Cost-to-Value Estimating Worksheet

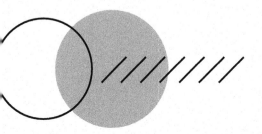

Impact Hypothesis Framework

Use this blank hypothesis framework to storyboard your chain of evidence from the expected change in knowledge, skills, and mindset to the short- and long-term effects of the program.

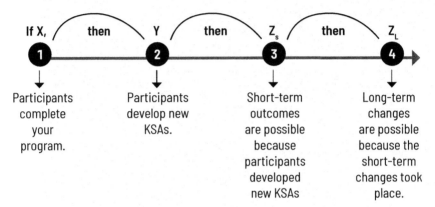

Participants complete your program.	Participants develop new KSAs.	Short-term outcomes are possible because participants developed new KSAs	Long-term changes are possible because the short-term changes took place.

Questions to Identify Your Hypothesis Variables

Ask these five essential questions from *Needs Assessment on a Shoestring* to discover the most important gaps your learning solution should address when you have limited time for an in-depth analysis:

- What is the most important thing that needs to change?
- What is currently driving the need for this change?
- What will happen if we don't solve the problem?
- If you could wave a magic wand, what is the one thing you would do to solve this problem?
- How will you know the problem is solved?

Learning Strategy Tracker

Use this blank template as inspiration for your learning strategy tracker. You should digitize it for easy searchability.

Status (Active, Complete, or In Development)	Program Name	Target Audience	KSA Goal	Short-Term Goal	Long-Term Goal

Measurement Map

Use this example measurement map for a sales training program to identify possible performance-focused leading indicators to monitor the effectiveness of your learning program.

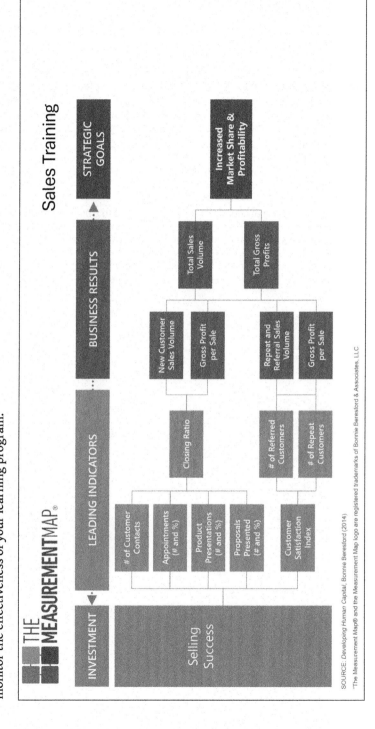

Sales Training

THE
MEASUREMENTMAP®

| INVESTMENT | LEADING INDICATORS | BUSINESS RESULTS | STRATEGIC GOALS |

Selling Success

- # of Customer Contacts
- Appointments (# and %)
- Product Presentations (# and %)
- Proposals Presented (# and %)
- Customer Satisfaction Index

Closing Ratio

# of Referred Customers

# of Repeat Customers

New Customer Sales Volume

Gross Profit per Sale

Repeat and Referral Sales Volume

Gross Profit per Sale

Total Sales Volume

Total Gross Profits

Increased Market Share & Profitability

SOURCE: *Developing Human Capital*, Bonnie Beresford (2014)

®The Measurement Map® and the Measurement Map logo are registered trademarks of Bonnie Beresford & Associates, LLC

Question Criteria Checklist

Use this checklist to build evaluation survey questions. The right questions check the following boxes:

❏	Questions are written to provide data showing whether the program accomplished its goals.
❏	Questions are predominantly closed-ended (except for cases when you are intentionally looking for narrative responses).
❏	Questions are worded clearly and objectively (not leading the responder to answer a certain way).
❏	Questions are asked at the right time for you to track growth or change.
❏	Questions are formatted to easily observe insights you need from the data.
❏	Questions will generate actionable feedback to improve future programs.

Self-Reported Evaluation Behavior Change Evaluation Plan

Before you begin, use this checklist to determine if your learning program is suited for a self-reported behavior change evaluation plan:

❏	My program taught participants new habits, tactics, activities, or behaviors.
❏	We communicated clear criteria or expectations with participants during their learning experience and they know what good and great examples of the new habits, tactics, activities, or behaviors look like.
❏	We gave participants at least three opportunities to practice the new habits, tactics, activities, or behaviors during their learning experience.
❏	Participants received at least one form of feedback when they practiced their new habits, tactics, activities, or behaviors during their learning experience.

If you checked three or four of the boxes, your program is suitable for a self-reported behavior change evaluation plan. If you checked two or fewer boxes, your program is not eligible. Participants must receive clear communication around behavior change expectations and must be given the chance to practice with feedback to have an accurate sense of the degree to which their behaviors may have changed.

Self-Reported Behavior Change Evaluation Plan:

1. Make a complete list of the habits, tactics, actions, or behaviors your program is designed to influence.
2. For each action, clarify one to three microbehavior changes you want to see as a result of your development program. Use an "I" statement for each microbehavior. For example:
   - **New habit:** empathetic listening
   - **Microbehavior expectation:** When I listen to someone's story or circumstances, I try to understand how they were feeling and what they were experiencing in that situation.
3. Populate your microbehavior "I" statements into a matrix with a 5-point Likert scale from agree to disagree.
4. Before your program begins, have each participant complete the matrix questionnaire.

5. Populate each statement into a new matrix that asks participants to rate their level of confidence implementing the behaviors back on the job with a 5-point Likert scale from very confident to not very confident.

6. During the last class, e-learning module, or virtual meeting, ask participants to complete the matrix questionnaire reflecting on their confidence performing the microbehaviors back on the job.

7. Show the results of the group's answers anonymously and engage in a discussion around what support would make participants feel more confident and what support they currently have that makes them feel confident.

8. Translate the prematrix questionnaire into a survey. Have the questions populate one at a time.

9. Two to four weeks after the program is over, gather your trainees for a postprogram check-in and have them complete the postprogram questionnaire.

10. Show the results of the group's answers anonymously and engage in a discussion around what factors help them practice certain behaviors frequently, as well as what gets in the way of practicing other behaviors more frequently.

11. Use the quantitative results to track changes in growth between pre- and postprogram questionnaires.

12. Use the data gathered in discussions to improve the support systems you create for future training participants.

Data Triangulation Exercise

To check if your dataset meets the basic requirements of triangulation, complete the following exercise. Give yourself one point for every true statement in the checklist.

Statement	True or False
My dataset contains qualitative (narrative) data.	
My dataset contains quantitative (numerical) data.	
My dataset contains information collected via direct observation.	
My dataset contains information collected via survey.	
My dataset contains information collected via interviews or focus groups.	
My dataset comes from a database (e.g., an HRM, LXP, CRM, or a sales enablement platform).	
My dataset comes from a social media or group communication platform (e.g., LinkedIn, Facebook, Slack, or Microsoft Teams).	
My dataset comes from a third-party vendor's assessment tool (e.g., standardized test scores, aptitude tests, or personality tests).	
My dataset comes from somewhere else that is not listed here.	

Note: Your goal is to have a minimum of three points when you calculate all your true statements, not to mark every statement as true. More data is not necessarily better—especially for professionals working on a shoestring. You reap the benefits of triangulation with three different data sources or types. Having more triangulation likely reaches its maximum benefit around five or six different data sources or types.

Data Triangulation Strategy Checklists

Use these checklists to make better data triangulation decisions.

Triangulation Strategy 1. Vary Data Types
- Include narrative (qualitative) data.
- Include numerical (quantitative) data.

Triangulation Strategy 2. Vary Data Sources (Use three sources.)
- Academic research published in peer-reviewed journals
- Research reports produced by credible associations, institutions, government agencies, and organizations, such as the Association for Talent Development (ATD), Deloitte, the Josh Bersin Company, RedThread Research, Society for Human Resource Management (SHRM), and the Brandon Hall Group.
- Assessment tools purchased from third-party evaluation vendors that assess growth in performance, capabilities, attitudes, personality, and knowledge, including the Intercultural Development Inventory (which assesses intercultural competence), the DiSC Assessment (which assesses personality traits), StrengthsFinder (which assesses individual capabilities), and the SAT, MAT, and LSAT (which are some of the most familiar knowledge assessments)
- Self-reported data from survey tools you create yourself, such as the self-reported assessment tool example that I developed with Larry Mohl to evaluate growth in inclusivity (chapter 3), exit survey data you might receive from your HR department, or employee engagement survey data
- Performance reviews
- Observational data you may receive when managers listen in on customer service team members' phone calls, when secret shoppers enter retail stores, or when principals observe and evaluate teachers
- Social communication data, including comments and posts shared on social media or in Slack conversations or questions input into chatbots
- Business intelligence data reporting progress on KPIs, such as sales, revenue, customer service reviews, customer retention, or operational efficiency

- Learning activity data, including how many times content was downloaded, clicked, or viewed, how much time learners spent listening to or viewing content, and attendance rates (which are often found on LMS and LXP platforms)
- Performance activity data telling you what employees are doing on the job, such as number of outbound sales calls and calls converted into sales, policies and procedures followed, and productivity quotas met

Results and Gaps Template

Use this template from *Partner for Performance* to create targets for your next training initiative.

Results	Indicators	Target	Current	Gap
Desired results of the stakeholders and organization	Data we'll track to measure progress	Where we'd like to be	Where we are currently	The difference between
Value-Add Results				
Organizational Results				
Operational Results				
Learning Results				

Source: Guerra-López and Hicks 2017.

Build It or Buy It Cost-to-Value Estimating Worksheet

Use this worksheet to map out your decision-making process to determine whether you should buy external support.

Build It		Buy It	
What are the initial costs to consider? • • •	Cost estimate:	What are the initial costs to consider? • • •	Cost estimate:
How much time will you need before you can begin using a minimum viable product (MVP)?	Time estimate:	How much time will you need before you can begin using a minimum viable product (MVP)?	Time estimate:
What is your initial cost to value ratio? (Total initial costs divided by time to MVP)	Cost-to-value ratio:	What is your initial cost to value ratio? (Total initial costs divided by time to MVP)	Cost-to-value ratio:
What are the monthly or annual costs to consider? • • •	Cost estimate:	What are the monthly or annual costs to consider? • • •	Cost estimate:
What is the short-term value? • • •	What is the estimated dollar value of these short-term outcomes?	What is the short-term value? • • •	What is the estimated dollar value of these short-term outcomes?
What is the long-term value? • • •	What is the estimated dollar value of these long-term outcomes?	What is the long-term value? • • •	What is the estimated dollar value of these long-term outcomes?

Build It		Buy It	
Calculate your total initial and monthly costs, and compare that to the total estimated dollar amount of value by adding the short- and long-term value estimates together.	What is the ratio? • 1:1* • 1:2** • 2:1***	Calculate your total initial and monthly costs, and compare that to the total estimated dollar amount of value by adding the short- and long-term value estimates together.	What is the ratio? • 1:1 • 1:2 • 2:1

*If your ratio is 1:1 in both columns, answer the additional questions to consider.

**If your ratio is 1:2, this indicates you are getting a lot of value compared to the investment, equating to a good investment.

***If your ratio is 2:1, your cost of investment is much greater than the estimated value in return. I suggest answering the additional questions to consider if the investment is worth the value.

Additional questions to consider if your ratio is 1:1 or 2:1

1. Do you have the time necessary to build both the expertise and the product you need to achieve the desired outcomes?
2. If you build the expertise and the product yourself, will you create a product with the minimum viable quality to achieve the desired outcomes?
3. Does investing the time to build the expertise and product yourself set you up for success for future projects? Or will this expertise or product only be used for one project or in rare instances?

References

Actionable. 2022. *2022 Annual Insights Report*. Toronto: Actionable.

Adams, R.E., R.L. Hogan, L.J. Steinke. 2020. *DACUM: The Designer's Guide to Curriculum Development*. Wilmington, DE: Edwin and Associates.

Alele, F., and B. Malau-Aduli. 2023. *An Introduction to Research Methods for Undergraduate Health Profession Students*. Townsville, QLD, Australia: James Cook University. jcu.pressbooks.pub/intro-res-methods-health /chapter/5-6-triangulation-of-data.

Anderson, V. 2007. *The Value of Learning: From Return on Investment to Return on Expectation*. London: Chartered Institute of Personnel and Development.

ATD (Association for Talent Development). 2009. *The Value of Evaluation: Making Training Evaluations More Effective*. Alexandria, VA: ATD Press.

ATD (Association for Talent Development). 2016. *Evaluating Learning: Getting to Measurements That Matter*. Alexandria, VA: ATD Press.

ATD (Association for Talent Development). 2023. *Measuring Impact: Using Data to Understand Learning Programs*. Alexandria, VA: ATD Press.

Baldwin, T.T., J.K. Ford, and B. Blume. 2009. "Transfer of Training 1988–2008: An Updated Review and New Agenda for Future Research." *International Review of Industrial and Organizational Psychology* 24:64–88. doi.org/10.1002 /9780470745267.ch2.

Beresford, B. n.d. "The Measurement Map." themeasurementmap.com.

Bersin, J. 2022. *HR Predictions for 2022*. Oakland, CA: The Josh Bersin Company. joshbersin.com/hr-predictions-for-2022.

Binder, C. 2017. "What It Really Means to Be Accomplishment Based." *Performance Improvement* 56(4): 20–25. doi.org/10.1002/pfi.21702.

Boulmetis, J., and P. Dutwin. 2011. *The ABCs of Evaluation: Timeless Techniques for Program and Project Managers*, 3rd ed. San Franscisco, CA: Jossey-Bass.

Brandon Hall Group. 2018. *Learning Measurement Impact on Business Results.* Delray Beach, FL: Brandon Hall Group.

Brandon Hall Group. 2020. *In Search of Impact: The State of Learning Measurement.* Delray Beach, FL: Brandon Hall Group.

Chui, M., E. Hazan, R. Roberts, A. Singla, K. Smaje, A. Sukharevsky, L. Yee, and R. Zemmel. 2023. *The Economic Potential of Generative AI: The Next Productivity Frontier.* Houston, TX: McKinsey and Company. mckinsey.com/capabilities /mckinsey-digital/our-insights/The-economic-potential-of-generative -AI-The-next-productivity-frontier#introduction.

Clark, R.C., and R.E. Mayer. 2023. *E-Learning and the Science of Instruction: Proven Guidelines for Consumers and Designers of Multimedia Learning,* 5th ed. Newark, NJ: John Wiley and Sons.

Conroy, R.M. 2018. *The RCSI Sample Size Handbook.* Dublin, Ireland: Royal College of Surgeons in Ireland. doi.org/10.13140/RG.2.2.30497.51043.

DataCamp. 2023. *The State of Data Literacy 2023.* New York: DataCamp. datacamp.com/blog/introducing-state-of-data-literacy-report.

Dillon, JD. 2022. *The Modern Learning Ecosystem: A New L&D Mindset for the Ever-Changing Workplace.* Alexandria, VA: ATD Press.

Dirksen, J. 2015. *Design for How People Learn,* 2nd ed. Hoboken, NJ: New Riders.

Dirksen, J. 2023. *Talk to the Elephant: Design Learning for Behavior Change.* San Francisco, CA: New Riders.

Dolfing, H. 2020. "Project Inputs, Activities, Outputs, Outcomes, Impact, and Results." Henrico Dolfing Blog, September 27. henricodolfing.com/2020 /09/project-inputs-outputs-outcomes.html.

Gartner, n.d. "data literacy (n.)." gartner.com/en/information-technology /glossary/data-literacy.

González-Calatayud, V., P. Prendes-Espinosa, and R. Roig-Vila. 2021. "Artificial Intelligence for Student Assessment: A Systematic Review." *Applied Science* 11(12): 5467. doi.org/10.3390/app11125467.

Guerra-López, I. 2013. "Performance Indicator Maps: A Visual Tool for Understanding, Managing, and Continuously Improving Your Business Metrics." *Performance Improvement* 52(6): 11–17. doi.org/10.1002/pfi.21373.

Guerra-López, I., and K. Hicks. 2017. *Partner for Performance: Strategically Aligning Learning and Development.* Alexandria, VA: ATD Press.

Harless, J. 1998. *The Eden Conspiracy: Educating for Accomplished Citizenship.* Wheaton, IL: Guild V Publications.

IBM Data and AI Team. 2023. "AI vs. Machine Learning vs. Deep Learning vs. Neural Networks: What's the Difference?" IBM Blog, July 6. ibm.com/blog /ai-vs-machine-learning-vs-deep-learning-vs-neural-networks.

Insights for Professionals (IFP). 2023. *The State of Learning and Development in 22/23.* Insights for Professionals. insightsforprofessionals.com/hr/learning -and-development/learning-development-research-report.

James, D. 2016. "Four Design Principles That Impact Performance Every Day." The Learning Guild, July 11. learningguild.com/articles/1997/four-design -principles-that-impact-performance-every-day/?rd=1.

Jones, K.L., and J.N. Lumsden. 2023. *Needs Assessment on a Shoestring.* Alexandria, VA: ATD Press.

King, K. 2020. *The Skillsoft Learning and Talent Maturity Framework: A Path to Accelerate HR's Adaptability and Your Workforce's Agility.* Nashua, NH: Skillsoft. skillsoft.com/resources/white-papers/the-skillsoft-learning-and-talent -maturity-framework.

Kirkpatrick, J.D., and W. Kirkpatrick. 2016. *Kirkpatrick's Four Levels of Training Evaluation.* Alexandria, VA: ATD Press.

Lea, P., and D. Ells. 2022. *Measuring the Business Impact of Learning in 2022.* Franklin, TN: Watershed, LEO Learning, and GP Strategies. watershedlrs .com/resources/research/measuring-business-impact-learning-2022.

Learning Technologies Group. 2021. *A Human Framework for Reskilling: How the 5 Seismic Forces Persist in a Post-Pandemic World.* London: Learning Technologies Group. ltgplc.com/wp-content/uploads/2021/07/LTG_white _paper_A_Human_Framework_for_Reskilling_2021.pdf.

LinkedIn Learning. 2022. *Workplace Learning Report 2022.* Sunnyvale, CA: LinkedIn Learning. learning.linkedin.com/content/dam/me/learning /resources/pdfs/linkedIn-learning-workplace-learning-report-2022.pdf.

LinkedIn Learning. 2023. *Workplace Learning Report 2023.* Sunnyvale, CA: LinkedIn Learning. learning.linkedin.com/content/dam/me/learning /en-us/pdfs/workplace-learning-report/LinkedIn-Learning_Workplace -Learning-Report-2023-EN.pdf.

LinkedIn Learning. 2024. *Workplace Learning Report 2024*. Sunnyvale, CA: LinkedIn Learning. learning.linkedin.com/content/dam/me/business /en-us/amp/learning-solutions/images/wlr-2024/LinkedIn-Workplace -Learning-Report-2024.pdf.

Mehrotra, P. 2019. "Learning Impact: Anything New?" Woodside, CA: RedThread Research, March 8. redthreadresearch.com/learning-impact -literature-review-2-2.

Mercer Mettl. 2022. *The State of Learning and Development 2022*. New York: Mercer Mettl. resources.mettl.com/research/state-of-learning-and-development -report-2022.

Mind Tools for Business. 2023a. *2023 Annual L&D Benchmark Report Part 1: Learning and Development in Organizations: Reflecting on 20 Years of Research*. Edinburgh, Scotland: Mind Tools. mindtools.com/business/research/20 -years-of-research.

Mind Tools for Business. 2023b. *2023 Annual L&D Benchmark Report Part 2: Unlocking Excellence: The Strategic Business Alignment Blueprint for L&D*. Edinburgh, Scotland: Mind Tools. mindtools.com/business/research /unlocking-excellence.

Mind Tools for Business. 2023c. *2023 Annual L&D Benchmark Report Part 3: Megatrends Reshaping the Future: The Crucial Role of L&D in Business Transformation*. Edinburgh, Scotland: Mind Tools. mindtools.com /business/research/megatrends-reshaping-the-future.

Mooney, T., and R.O. Brinkerhoff. 2008. *Courageous Training: Bold Actions for Business Results*. San Francisco, CA: Berrett-Koehler Publishers.

Nelson, B. 2022. "Beyond The Buzzword: What Does Data-Driven Decision-Making Really Mean?" *Forbes*, September 22. forbes.com/sites/tableau /2022/09/23/beyond-the-buzzword-what-does-data-driven-decision -making-really-mean/?sh=2a3fc1b125d6.

Newbauer, K. 2023. *Aligning Instructional Design With Business Goals: Make the Case and Deliver Results*. Alexandria, VA: ATD Press.

NovoEd. 2023. *Cohort Learning in the Age of AI*. San Fransisco, CA: NovoEd. novoed.com/resources/insights/cohort-learning-in-the-age-of-ai.

Pease, G., B. Beresford, and L. Walker. 2014. *Developing Human Capital: Using Analytics to Plan and Optimize Your Learning and Development Investment*. Hoboken, NJ: Wiley.

Pew Research Center. 2024. "Social Media Fact Sheet." Pew Research Center. pewresearch.org/internet/fact-sheet/social-media.

Phillips, J. 2010. "Confronting CEO Expectations About the Value of Learning." *TD*, January 14. td.org/magazines/td-magazine/confronting-ceo -expectations-about-the-value-of-learning.

Robinson, D.G., J.C. Robinson, J.J. Phillips, P.P. Phillips, and D. Handshaw. 2015. *Performance Consulting: A Strategic Process to Improve, Measure, and Sustain Organizational Results*, 3rd ed. Oakland, CA: Berrett-Koehler Publishers.

Rogers, E.M. 2003. *Diffusion of Innovations*, 5th ed. New York: Free Press.

Steinbrinck, K. 2023. "The History of Email: Digging Into the Past, Present, and Future." Email on Acid Blog, November 30. emailonacid.com/blog/article /email-marketing/history-of-email.

Szlachta, A. 2022. "Know Your Value: How to Measure the Outcomes and Impact of Learning." Session at ATD's Core 4 Conference. San Antonio, TX, July 18–19.

TalentLMS. *What Employees Want From L&D in 2024*. San Fransisco: TalentLMS. talentlms.com/research/learning-development-trends#:~:text =The%20top%203%20non-mandatory,and%20use%20of%20AI%20tools.

Talent LMS and Society for Human Resource Management (SHRM). 2022. *2022 Workplace Learning and Development Trends: Research Report*. San Francisco, CA: Talent LMS. talentlms.com/employee-learning-and-development -stats.

Tannenbaum, S., J.E. Methieu, J. Cannon-Bowers, and E. Salas. 1993. *Factors That Influence Training Effectiveness: A Conceptual Model and Longitudinal Analysis*. Technical Report 93-001. Orlando, FL: Naval Air Warfare Center, Training Systems Division. apps.dtic.mil/sti/tr/pdf/ADA306933.pdf.

Taylor, D.H. 2024. *L&D Global Sentiment Survey 2024*. London: Donald H. Taylor. donaldhtaylor.co.uk/research_base/global-sentiment-survey-2024.

Thalheimer, W. 2018. "One of the Biggest Lies in Learning Evaluation." Work- Learning Research Blog, January 18. worklearning.com/2018/01/18/one -of-the-biggest-lies-in-learning-evaluation-asking-learners-about-level -3-and-4.

Torrance, M. 2023. *Data and Analytics for Instructional Designers*. Alexandria, VA: ATD Press.

Vance, D., and P. Parskey. 2020. *Measurement Demystified: Creating Your L&D Measurement, Analytics, and Reporting Strategy.* Alexandria, VA: ATD Press.

Vance, D., and P. Parskey. 2021. *Measurement Demystified Field Guide.* Alexandria, VA: ATD Press.

Watershed. 2022. *Adopting Learning Analytics: Closing the C-Suite/L&D Language Gap.* Franklin, TN: Watershed. watershedlrs.com/resources/research /adopting-learning-analytics-c-suite-l-and-d-language-gap.

Yates, K.M. n.d. "L&D Detective." kevinmyates.com.

Index

About the Author

 An academic turned entrepreneur, **Alaina Szlachta, PhD,** is the founder of By Design Development Solutions, a consulting firm specializing in data enablement. Drawing on her background as a researcher and public health educator, she partners with learning and operations teams to integrate measurement and evaluation systems into their daily practices, providing continuous feedback loops that enhance quality, efficiency, and profitability.

Alaina brings a wealth of experience to her work. Her diverse client portfolio spans higher education, diversity and inclusion, finance, victim services, real estate, healthcare, and SaaS. She holds a bachelor's degree in communication and marketing from Seattle University, as well as master's and doctorate degrees in education and health education from Widener University.

Alaina's passion lies in culturally responsive teaching, demonstrating the value of learning through data enablement, designing curricula that facilitate behavior change, and championing excellence in education. She generously shares her expertise through writing, speaking engagements, and as the host of Measurement Made Easy, a free community of practice that guides practitioners in refining their impact measurement strategies.

When not revolutionizing data practices, Alaina can be found exploring her adopted hometown of Austin, Texas, where she embraces an active lifestyle, running and kayaking around the scenic Lady Bird Lake.

To learn more about Alaina and to sign up to her newsletter The Weekly Measure, visit dralainaszlachta.com.

About ATD

atd The Association for Talent Development (ATD) is the world's largest association dedicated to those who develop talent in organizations. Serving a global community of members, customers, and international business partners in more than 100 countries, ATD champions the importance of learning and training by setting standards for the talent development profession.

Our customers and members work in public and private organizations in every industry sector. Since ATD was founded in 1943, the talent development field has expanded significantly to meet the needs of global businesses and emerging industries. Through the Talent Development Capability Model, education courses, certifications and credentials, memberships, industry-leading events, research, and publications, we help talent development professionals build their personal, professional, and organizational capabilities to meet new business demands with maximum impact and effectiveness.

One of the cornerstones of ATD's intellectual foundation, ATD Press offers insightful and practical information on talent development, training, and professional growth. ATD Press publications are written by industry thought leaders and offer anyone who works with adult learners the best practices, academic theory, and guidance necessary to move the profession forward.

We invite you to join our community. Learn more at **TD.org**.